W9-BIA-362

THE SALEM WITCHCRAFT TRIALS

A Headline Court Case

Geraldine Woods

Enslow Publishers, Inc.

40 Industrial Road
Box 398
Berkeley Heights, NJ 07922
USA

PO Box 38
Aldershot
Hants GU12 6BP
UK

http://www.enslow.com

Library of Congress Cataloging-in-Publication Data

Woods, Geraldine.
    The Salem witchcraft trials: a headline court case / Geraldine Woods.
       p. cm.—(Headline court cases)
    Includes bibliographical references and index.
    Summary: Examines the events surrounding the Salem Witchcraft
Trials and the unjust treatment of those who were falsely accused.
    ISBN 0-7660-1383-9
    1. Trials (Witchcraft)—Massachusetts—Salem Juvenile literature.
2. Salem (Mass.)—History Juvenile literature. [1. Trials (Witchcraft)
—Massachusetts—Salem. 2. Witchcraft—Massachusetts—Salem.
3. Salem (Mass.)—History—Colonial period, ca. 1600–1775.]
I. Title. II. Series.
KFM2478.8.W5W66   2000
345.744'50288—dc21   99-37773
                                            CIP

Printed in the United States of America

10 9 8 7 6 5 4 3

To Our Readers: We have done our best to make sure all Internet addresses in this book
were active and appropriate when we went to press. However, the author and the publisher
have no control over and assume no liability for the material available on those Internet
sites or on other Web sites they may link to. Any comments or suggestions can be sent by
e-mail to comments@enslow.com or to the address on the back cover.

Photo Credits: Courtesy Peabody Essex Museum, Salem, MA, pp. 1, 10, 14,
19, 24, 36, 38, 44, 46, 53, 58, 71; Danvers Archival Center, pp. 6, 16, 22; Library
of Congress, p. 72; © Richard B. Trask, p. 87.

Cover Photo: "The Trial of George Jacobs, August 5, 1692" oil on Canvas by
T. H. Matteson, 1855, Courtesy Peabody Essex Museum, Salem, MA.

Contents

═══ Headline Court Cases ═══

The Andersonville Prison Civil War Crimes Trial
A Headline Court Case
0-7660-1386-3

The John Brown Slavery Revolt Trial
A Headline Court Case
0-7660-1385-5

The Lindbergh Baby Kidnapping Trial
A Headline Court Case
0-7660-1389-8

The Lizzie Borden "Axe Murder" Trial
A Headline Court Case
0-7660-1422-3

The Nuremberg Nazi War Crimes Trial
A Headline Court Case
0-7660-1384-7

The Sacco and Vanzetti Controversial Murder Trial
A Headline Court Case
0-7660-1387-1

The Salem Witchcraft Trials
A Headline Court Case
0-7660-1383-9

The Scopes Monkey Trial
A Headline Court Case
0-7660-1388-X

chapter one

WITCHES ON TRIAL

SALEM VILLAGE—"An Army of Devils is horribly broke in upon . . . the Houses of the Good People there are fill'd with the . . . shrieks of their Children and Servants. . . ."[1]

Rebecca Nurse was old, sick, and nearly deaf. Yet in the minds of some people in the Massachusetts Bay Colony, she was one of the most dangerous people they could imagine. The date was June 30, 1692. Rebecca "Goody" Nurse was a seventy-one-year-old great-grandmother who lived in Salem Village, a two- to three-hour walk from Salem Town. Together with her husband, Francis Nurse, Goody Nurse had raised eight children and farmed the rocky soil of New England. ("Goody" is short for "goodwife," the title of some respect given to married women of average status in the Puritan community.) Until April, her life had been filled with prayer, hard work, and family. But now she was on trial in a Salem courtroom. The charge was witchcraft.

At the front of the courtroom sat the judges. They were respected members of the community who had been appointed by Governor William Phips to this special Court of Oyer and Terminer, the court of hearing and deciding. Though none of them had formal legal training, the judges had studied the basis of all law in Salem—the Bible. They knew that the Bible ordered, "There shall not be found among you any one that uses divination [fortune telling], or an enchanter, or a witch."[2]

The Chief Justice of the court was William Stoughton, a stern man who believed, as did most people in Salem, that the devil enlisted human beings to do his work on earth. Stoughton was joined by John Hathorne (an ancestor of Nathaniel Hawthorne, the famous American writer), Jonathan Corwin, and others. To the judges, it was entirely possible that the woman in front of them could summon the power of the devil—even in the courtroom. To protect the innocent, guards stood on each side of Goody Nurse. She was told to look only at the judges to make

William Stoughton, the Chief Justice of the Court of Oyer and Terminer, believed, as did most people in Salem, that the devil enlisted the help of human beings on earth to do his work.

sure that an evil glance from her did not curse the person it fell upon.

Between the judges and Rebecca Nurse were some of her accusers. They were girls just entering their teens, along with a few older, married women. Throughout the trial, these accusers twisted themselves into strange positions and howled in pain because, they said, Goody Nurse was sticking them with pins and pinching them. True, Goody Nurse's body did not move. But the women said they were tormented by her specter, or spirit—something they said looked just like Rebecca Nurse, but was invisible to everyone but themselves.

Some of the accusers also gave evidence of past crimes they said Nurse had committed. One of those accusers was Ann Putnam, the wife of Thomas Putnam. Putnam had signed many of the complaints against witches. Goody Putnam was the mother of Ann Putnam, Jr., who also claimed to be tormented. Goody Putnam's life had been filled with tragedy. Born into a rich family, she received no inheritance when her father died. She sued his estate but lost. Three of her sister's newborn children and one of her own babies had died, and her sister, Goody Bayley, had also recently passed away. Ann Putnam herself was sickly. Now she testified that

> On the first day of June 1692 the apparition [spirit or ghost] of Rebecca Nurse did fall upon me and almost choked me. . . . She told me she had killed Benjamin Houlton and John Fuller and Rebecca Shepard. She also told me that she and her sister Cloyce had killed young John Putnam's child. Immediately there did appear to me six children in winding

sheets [burial clothes], which called me aunt, which did most grievously frighten me . . . also there appeared to me my own sister Bayley and three of her children in winding sheets and told me that Goody Nurse had murdered them.[3]

Eyewitnesses reported that Rebecca Nurse herself seemed shocked and confused by the whole proceeding. When she had first been questioned back in March, she was sick in bed and could not go out. She told her visitors that she was praying for the victims of witchcraft. However, she also said she was worried about the women who had been accused. "Some of the persons they have spoken of are," she said, "as innocent as I."[4] Informed of the charges against her, Goody Nurse said in amazement and sorrow, "I am as innocent as the child unborn."[5] Then she wondered if God was punishing her for something she had done, something that she had neglected to ask forgiveness for. "[W]hat sin hath God found out in me unrepented of that he should lay such an affliction [suffering] upon me in my old age?" she asked.[6]

Before her trial, Rebecca Nurse had undergone an embarrassing physical examination. Women appointed by the court had searched every inch of her body for the special mark of a witch, the "witch's teat." The teat, or nipple, was believed to be a sign that the devil placed on the witch's body when he or she signed his or her name in the devil's book and became a servant of evil.[7] The teat was also the spot on the witch's body where a ghostly animal could supposedly suck the witch's spirit. The ghostly animal, called the witch's familiar, was thought to participate in the witch's evil work. At Rebecca Nurse's examination, some of the examiners believed that they had discovered such a mark. However, one examiner said that she had found only ordinary warts or moles. Rebecca Nurse asked for a second examination, but her request was denied.[8]

Also in the courtroom were Rebecca Nurse's family and many of her friends. They were sure that she was innocent. In fact, thirty-nine of her neighbors had sent a petition to the court explaining that Goody Nurse was, in their eyes, a model of devotion to God and to the Puritan community. Though they did not say so in their petition, some of Nurse's supporters may have thought that the "victims" themselves were under the influence of the devil.[9]

At least one person in the courtroom saw the accusers as frauds—clever actresses seeking attention or the downfall of their families' enemies. Rebecca Nurse's daughter Sarah, watching carefully, told the court that during the trial she had seen one of the accusers, Goody Bibber, "pull pins out of her [clothes] and held them between her fingers and claspt her hands round her knees and then she cried out and said Goody Nurse pinched her."[10]

But the judges ignored Sarah. So Rebecca Nurse's supporters were worried. If the accusers could convince the jury that their suffering was real, and that Rebecca Nurse had caused it, Nurse might be found guilty. The crime of witchcraft was punishable by death.

Some spectators must also have wondered who would be next. By the time Goody Nurse went on trial, over fifty people from Salem and the surrounding area were in jail on the same charges, and more people were being named as witches every day. Some of the accused were the outcasts of the community; people who had always seemed a little odd. But if Goody Nurse could be accused of witchcraft, apparently no one in Salem was safe from that charge.

After hearing evidence, the jury was sent out to consider its verdict. The crowded room was silent as the jury returned and faced the judges. Goody Nurse, the jury declared, was not guilty. Immediately, the accusers screamed even louder than before and moved their bodies into even stranger positions. The spectators must have been wondering if this new

Suspected witches were required to submit to an embarrassing physical examination. Women appointed by the court would search every inch of the accused witch's body in search of the special mark of a witch, the "witch's teat."

suffering was a sign that the verdict was wrong. Could the devil have triumphed? Or could it be more trickery?

Chief Justice William Stoughton solemnly asked the jury members if they had considered one important piece of evidence. When Deliverance Hobbs, a self-confessed witch, came in to testify, Goody Nurse had seemed surprised and said, "She is one of us."[11] Stoughton interpreted Nurse's comment to mean "one of us witches." To Stoughton, this comment proved Nurse's guilt. He asked the jury to leave the room again in order to reconsider its verdict.

A short time later the jury members returned, but not with a decision. They wanted to ask Goody Nurse what she had meant by her remark. But Nurse was tired and sad. The noise and commotion in the courtroom had probably distracted her, and she may not have heard the question. She said nothing at all. The jury went out again, and the crowd waited.[12]

History waited also. Though the Puritans in the courtroom did not know it, the trials they conducted would become some of the most famous in American history. Before they were over, 165 people would be accused in Salem, and twenty were condemned.[13] The entire community would be torn apart both during the trials and after, as the Puritans of Salem asked themselves the question that historians are still trying to answer: Why did the Salem witch trials take place?

chapter two

A RELIGIOUS COLONY

NEW ENGLAND—"We shall be as a City upon a Hill, the eyes of all People are upon us: so that if we shall deal falsely with our God in this work we have undertaken . . . [we shall] cause him to withdraw his present help from us."[1]

The founder of the Massachusetts Bay Colony, Minister John Winthrop, arrived in North America on a religious mission. His "City Upon a Hill" was to be an ideal society, governed not by political ideas or economics, but by religious principles. As another minister, John Higginson, said in a sermon, "New England is originally a plantation of religion, not a plantation of trade."[2] Winthrop's group wanted to live in a society organized completely around plain living, devotion to God, and the rules of the Bible. Winthrop and his followers were technically part of the Church of England, but they disagreed with some of its beliefs. Because they wanted to reform the Church of England and make it purer, they were called Puritans.

In seventeenth-century England, disagreement often meant persecution. Some Puritans were arrested and tortured; others had their property taken away by the government. It was clear to the Puritans that they would never be able to worship in their own way if they stayed in Europe. So the Puritans bought all of the stock in the Massachusetts Bay Company, which had established trading colonies in North America. By 1640 there were some fifteen thousand Puritans in New England. Boston, Salem, and Falmouth (now Portland, Maine) were some of the important Puritan settlements. The colony prospered.

Salem Town, with a good harbor and many rivers, quickly became an important trading and fishing center. However, its soil was poor. In the late 1630s, settlers moved west of the town, where land was much more fertile. They established a farming village that supplied food for Salem Town.

Officially, Salem Village, also called the Farms, was part of Salem Town. Residents paid taxes to the town, and they were required to send men to stand guard duty in the town's militia. However, as the farms grew, many of Salem's villagers wanted to break away from Salem Town. Several times the Farmers sent petitions to the colonial government in Boston for permission to establish their own institutions—their own meetinghouse, their own guard duty, and so forth. They also asked to be released from obligations to Salem Town. In 1667, for example, the Farmers wrote that "Some of us live ten miles, some eight or nine; the nearest are at least five miles from Salem meeting-house (upon the road)—and then 'tis nearly a mile farther to the sentry-place . . . so that some of us must travel armed eleven miles to watch . . . And yet [we are] not excused from paying our part" in Salem Town's taxes.[3] The colonial government ruled that men who lived more than four miles from the town did not have to do guard duty. In 1672, the Salem villagers received permission to build their own meetinghouse and to hire a minister. In 1689, the villagers were finally allowed to establish an independent church. In 1692, however, Salem Village was still not completely

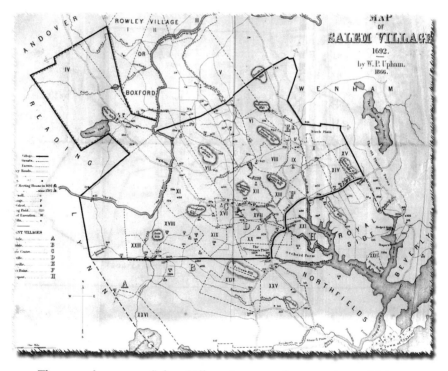

The area known as Salem Village is mapped out as it would have appeared in 1692.

independent, and there was a great deal of tension between the town and the Farms.

Only about fifty adults out of a population of some five hundred were full members of the Salem Village church.[4] The Puritans believed that from the moment of birth, everyone's fate was already decided by God. Only a few were destined for heaven, and everyone else would spend eternity in hell. Good deeds and righteous living could not change one's fate. However, the community might be able to recognize a person's fate by the way he or she behaved. The Puritan Church only voted full membership to people who professed this faith. Those selected for this honor were said to be "visible saints." People who had not proved their holiness were members of the congregation but not the church. They attended services, paid taxes to support the minister, and followed church rules. However, they were not allowed to vote on church business. During services, worshippers sat in assigned pews. The church members sat in the front, ranked in order of wealth and social position. They often had a special service, just for themselves, after the rest of the congregation was dismissed.

A Strict Way of Life

The privileges of full church membership extended into the government of the colony. Originally, the Puritan government was a theocracy. That is, the government and the Puritan religion were intertwined. Only male members of the church were allowed to vote and hold public office. The highest governing body was the General Court, which combined some of the duties of a Congress and a Supreme Court. The General Court passed laws and heard appeals from lower courts. When the General Court itself needed advice on a point of law, they turned to Puritan ministers for an opinion. In 1662, King Charles II sent a letter to the Massachusetts Bay Colony, ordering "freedom and liberty of conscience" for all residents. He said that people of

THE FIRST MEETING HOUSE, 1673 - 1701

In 1672, the villagers of Salem received permission to build their own meetinghouse and to hire a minister.

different religions "may have their votes in the election of all officers, both civil and military."[5] The General Court delayed the effects of the king's ruling as long as possible. First, the court waited three years before announcing the king's letter to the colony. Then the letter was ignored wherever possible. By 1692, the Massachusetts Bay Colony was no longer a legal theocracy. However, in practice male Puritan church members still held most of the power.

Like all Englishmen, the Puritans did not believe, as we do, that defendants in criminal cases are innocent until proven guilty. Nor did they think that defendants needed a lawyer, although defendants were allowed to call witnesses and to question those testifying against them. If the defendants were innocent, the Puritans thought, God would reveal the truth. Defendants were often urged to confess, even before all the evidence was in. Hanging was the sentence for many crimes. Those convicted of lesser offenses might be whipped, have their ears or noses slit open, or have a burning brand placed on their hands or cheeks. Sometimes wrongdoers were ordered to spend a day in the town square, locked in stocks. Stocks were wooden frames that held the prisoner's legs.[6] The Puritans punished many activities that today we would not consider crimes: scolding, speaking against the Church, and sleeping during religious services were all punishable offenses.[7]

Witchcraft was an especially feared crime. The Puritans believed that a witch could, through supernatural means, bring serious harm or even death to people and animals. Spells, magical objects, or invisible spirits, the Puritans thought, could cause such misfortunes as a sick cow, a failed crop, or the sudden death of a perfectly healthy person. The witch drew on the power of the devil to do these evil deeds, the Puritans said.[8]

On Sundays, all nonreligious activity was illegal, and everyone was expected to attend church. The service, or meeting, lasted for three hours in the morning. After a dinner break, it continued for two more hours. During the service an official of the church walked among the congregation with a stick, prodding anyone who was not paying attention. Few amusements were permitted because the Puritans thought that anything but work and prayer was a possible invitation to sin. One of the complaints against Bridget Bishop, one of the accused Salem witches, was that she "did entertain people in her house at unseasonable hours in the night to keep drinking and playing at shuffle-board, whereby discord [disagreement] did arise in other families, and young people were in danger to be corrupted [tempted to a life of sin]."[9]

A Legal Crisis

The Salem Village of 1692, along with the entire Massachusetts Bay Colony, was in a state of legal crisis. All of New England operated under a royal charter—official permission and a set of rules for the government of the colony—granted by the king of England. The king also appointed a governor to manage the colony. In the early years, this system worked well. However, England went through several political upheavals during the second half of the century. Problems across the sea quickly affected the Massachusetts Bay Colony. In 1684, the royal charter was taken away, and in 1686, the king appointed a new governor, Sir Edmund Andros. The colonists hated Andros because he took away some of their rights. When the government of England changed again in 1688, the colonists seized the

These Puritans are on their way to church. On Sundays, all nonreligious activity was illegal. Everyone was expected to attend church.

opportunity to overthrow Andros. For a while the colony ruled itself, but it was technically without a legal system. It needed a new charter from the British crown. A delegation of important Puritans, including the Reverend Increase Mather, the famous Boston minister, went to England in 1688 to negotiate for the colony.

When the accusations of witchcraft began, the colony's representatives were still in London. Massachusetts could hold hearings and imprison suspected wrongdoers, but serious crimes (like witchcraft) could not be officially tried without a legal court system in place. A legal bottleneck was created; witches could be accused, examined, and imprisoned, but no case could be completed.

Links to the Old Country

In their fears of witchcraft, the colonists were following a pattern established in the mother country. Between 1560 and 1760, Europe participated in what some historians have called a witchcraze. About one hundred thousand people, mostly women, were executed for the crime of witchcraft. In Germany alone, some thirty thousand accused witches were executed. Most New Englanders would have been aware of the witchcraze in Chelmsford, England, in the 1640s. Of the thirty-eight people put on trial in the Chelmsford area, twenty-nine were found guilty and executed. The Salem Village outbreak began just as the witchcraft trials in Europe were slowing down.

The New Englanders' beliefs about the nature of witchcraft followed English traditions. Besides witch's teats and familiars, the witch was said to fly on a stick and to sign the devil's book. Spells could be placed by casting the "evil eye" on the victim or by sticking pins in a little doll. Professional witchfinders used several methods to detect a witch. A witch was not supposed to be able to say the Lord's Prayer without error. Many witches were thrown into water, because the water was thought to reject an impure person. In testing witches, therefore, those who floated were guilty and those who sank were innocent. Some people drowned before they could be pulled out of the water—their good names, but not their lives, saved. The touch test was also popular. If someone under a spell touched the witch who had cast the spell, the suffering would stop because the curse would flow back from the victim into the witch.

One famous witchfinder, Matthew Hopkins of Essex, England, wrote a book in 1647 called *Discovery of Witches.* Hopkins said that suspected witches should be put on a stool and watched continuously. Eventually, Hopkins said, the witch's familiar would show up, or the witch would confess. Hopkins also walked suspected witches for days at a time, again waiting for a confession or a sign of guilt. Both these methods made the suspect go without sleep for very long periods. It is easy to imagine that some "witches" confessed simply because they were desperate for rest.[10]

The Puritans also thought that witches passed along their evil ways to those around them. Because witchcraft was associated mostly with females, a woman accused of witch-craft brought suspicion on her daughter, and in rare cases, on the men in the family as well. Today we tend to consider young children innocent, but the Puritans thought that it was possible to be born evil. Cotton Mather, the son of Increase Mather and also a minister, wrote that if children "are not too little to die, they are not too little to go to hell."[11]

Laws Against Witchcraft

Most of Salem's legal documents refer to the Old Testament of the Bible for explanations, authority, and guidance, particularly in criminal cases. However, the Puritans were also influenced by the laws of the country they had left behind. Before the sixteenth century, witchcraft was a religious, not a legal, issue in England unless it involved an attempt to overthrow the government. In 1542, King Henry VIII created the first English law against "conjura[t]ions [spells] and witchcraftes and sorcery and enchantments" designed to gain "unlawful love," discover stolen property, or to destroy a person in body or goods.[12] The penalty for a first offense was a year in prison; a second offense was usually punishable by death.[13] In 1604, King James I passed a law ordering that if "any person shall be [by witchcraft] killed,

A group of important Puritans, including the Reverend Increase Mather (shown here), went to England in 1688 to negotiate the establishment of a legal system for their colony.

destroyed, wasted . . . or lamed" the witch "shall suffer pains of death."[14] In 1641, the Massachusetts Bay Colony modeled its own law on that of King James. "If any man or woman be a witch . . . [and] consulteth with a familiar spirit . . . they shall be put to death."[15] When the colony lost its charter in 1684, all its own laws were suspended. The Salem judges brought charges according to the 1604 English law, but they had no legal courts to try the cases.

Early Witchcraft Prosecutions in New England

The first formal charge of witchcraft in the colonies was made in 1647. A year later, Margaret Jones became the first person to be executed for witchcraft in the Massachusetts Bay Colony. Jones was a healer and a midwife (someone who delivers babies but is not a doctor). Jones was reported to have had an argument with her neighbor and then "some mischief befel such Neighbors."[16] She was also charged with giving medicines that had violent effects. It was said that if a patient refused Jones's medicine, nothing else would cure the illness.[17] Jones's career put her in danger. According to historian John Demos, who analyzed trial records from all over colonial New England, healers and midwives ran a higher risk of being accused of witchcraft.[18] In fact, midwives had to swear that they would not use witchcraft in their work. The Puritans may have been afraid of the healers' power. The power to help could too easily become the power to hurt. One English Puritan writer, William Perkins, said that all healing from "wise men and wise women" came from the devil.[19]

Before 1692, many convicted witches received light punishments or simple warnings. Some accused witches were not charged at all. Elizabeth Knapp, for example, was a sixteen-year-old servant in the home of the Reverend Samuel Willard when she began to have fits in 1671. Cotton Mather reported that "her tongue for many hours together was drawn like a semicircle up to the roof of her mouth, not to be removed, though some tried with their fingers to do it."[20] Mather also said that "six men were scarce able to hold her in some of her fits."[21] Knapp shrieked and then burst into laughter when asked what was wrong. She complained of being strangled and tried to jump into a fire. Then Knapp accused a neighbor's specter of tormenting her. Willard said the neighbor was "a person of sincere uprightness before God" and did not file a complaint. As time went by, Knapp became more and more confused, at times saying that she

had given in to the devil's temptations and at other times saying that she had resisted. Willard came to believe that Elizabeth Knapp herself was possessed by the devil, and though he tried to cure her, he could not. However, no one was charged with a crime in the Knapp case.

Cotton Mather (shown here), was the son of Increase Mather. Like his father, Cotton Mather was a minister. He believed that it was possible for children to be born evil.

Mary Glover was not so lucky. She was one of about fifteen people executed for witchcraft between 1648—when the first "witch" was executed in the colonies—and the Salem outbreak.[22] In 1688, Mary Glover, an immigrant from Ireland, directed "very bad language" at Martha Goodwin. Soon Martha began to have fits, as did three other children in the family. When questioned, Mary Glover "had not power to deny her interest in the Enchantment of the Children."[23] Being Irish (and not having English as her first language), Glover may not have understood the questions put to her, or she may not have known how to defend herself in English. The magistrates did not know what to think; they wondered if she might be mad. However, after a doctor had testified that Mary Glover was sane, the magistrates handed down a death sentence. The Goodwin children did not recover when Glover died. Cotton Mather took Goodwin and her brother into his home to try to cure them with prayer. Eventually the children returned to normal.

The Glover case had some of the ingredients soon to emerge in Salem: suffering children, a foreign servant, and a minister confronting the devil. Cotton Mather claimed victory. The Reverend Samuel Parris, pastor of Salem Village, could not do the same.

chapter three

THE TROUBLE BEGINS

SALEM VILLAGE—" 'Tis horrible that in this land of uprightness, there should be any such Pranks of Wickedness."[1]

The Reverend Samuel Parris was not a peaceful man. Before he became minister of Salem Village in 1689, he had argued with the congregation for almost a year over salary and benefits, including the deed to the parsonage, the house the village provided for the minister. Parris won that battle, but he lost others. When he finally arrived in Salem, the parish was divided into two groups, those who favored Parris and those who thought he was the wrong man for the job. During his years in Salem Village, Parris did nothing to bring the two sides together. However, the division might not have been entirely his fault. Salem Village was in the habit of fighting. Two of its previous ministers, James Bayley and George Burroughs, had left in the midst of quarrels.[2]

The house that Parris fiercely wanted to own was a substantial two-story wooden building with two rooms on each floor, a half-cellar, and a shed. There was little privacy, because at least eight people lived in the parsonage. The head of the household, Samuel Parris, had been born in 1653. He was originally a merchant, but his business did not do well. Salem Village was his first parish. His wife, Elizabeth Parris, was often ill. The Parrises had a nine-year-old daughter, Betty, as well as a son and younger daughter who played no role in the witch trials. An eleven-year-old niece, Abigail Williams, also lived in the parsonage.

A slave couple, Tituba and John Indian, took care of the household chores and cared for the children. Historians do not know where Tituba was born. Some believe that she was an American Indian, captured in South America by slave traders. Others think that Tituba was born into the Yoruba tribe of West Africa. Parris took her with him to Massachusetts when he moved there in the early 1680s. During the witch trials, Tituba was probably between twenty and thirty years old. John Indian, as his name suggests, was probably an American Indian.

The winter of 1691–1692 was harsh. The parish records show that the Sunday service in the unheated meetinghouse had to be cut short several times "by reason of the Cold."[3]

According to Cotton Mather, by 1691 many young people in Massachusetts were being "led away [from goodness] with little sorceries."[4] Betty and Abigail, as well as some friends from nearby houses, were no exception. They tried to brighten the long winter days by fortune-telling. According to Reverend John Hale, who wrote about the witch trials soon after they ended, the girls wanted to know whom they would marry and "what trade their sweethearts should be of."[5] Tradition says that Tituba taught her young charges to make a crystal ball by breaking an egg into a glass of water. As the egg white drifted down, the girls stared at it and tried to find shapes. A tool shape might mean that the girl would marry a carpenter; a book shape might predict that her future husband would be a teacher or a minister. One day, the story goes, the girls saw "the likeness of a coffin" and began to scream.[6]

Whether or not this story is true, Betty and her cousin did become ill. They had terrible nightmares, and according to Robert Calef, another writer of the time, they took "odd postures" (body positions), made "foolish, ridiculous speeches," and began to have "fits."[7] In February 1692, Reverend Parris called in William Griggs, a local doctor. Griggs examined the girls, but he could not find a physical illness to explain their behavior. Today mental illness might be considered a cause, but in the seventeenth century, mental illness was neither recognized nor understood. Griggs's verdict was spiritual: The girls, he said, were "under an evil hand."[8] That is, witchcraft was involved.

Parris later said that he was terribly embarrassed that "the Lord ordered the late horrid calamity [disaster] . . . to break out first in my family."[9] The minister prayed and fasted, hoping to defeat the problem by religious means. He also called in two other ministers, Nicholas Noyes and John Hale, and asked their advice. They advised patience and more prayer, "to wait upon the providence [goodness] of God to see what time may discover."[10]

However, not everyone was content to wait. Mary Sibley, a neighbor, advised John Indian to check for witchcraft by baking a witch cake. John Indian was apparently told to mix cornmeal with some urine from the suffering girls and to feed the cake to a dog. According to Sibley, the dog would behave strangely if witchcraft were indeed the source of the problem.

No one knows whether the dog actually ate the cake. We do know that Parris found out about the plan and became very upset. In his view, all spells were evil, even those intended to fight another spell. He wrote that in the days after the witch cake was baked

> apparitions [ghosts] have been plenty, and exceeding much mischief hath followed. But by this means . . . the Devil hath been raised amongst us, and his rage is . . . terrible, and when he shall be silenced the Lord only knows.[11]

Instead of easing, the "illness" began to spread. Twelve-year-old Ann Putnam, seventeen-year-old Elizabeth Hubbard, Mercy Lewis (orphaned in a war with the American Indians), and others started to show symptoms. Deodat Lawson, a minister investigating the case, reported that Mary Walcott had mysterious bite marks on her arm. He also saw Abigail Williams pull burning logs from the fireplace in the parsonage and toss them around the room. Not only girls were affected; married women also began to act strangely. Goody Putnam, Ann Putnam's mother, had a "sore fit" that improved temporarily when Lawson prayed with her.[12]

The residents of Salem Village now looked at each other with suspicion. Many people remembered past misfortunes: milk that spoiled, a feverish child, a sudden pain. At the time they occurred, these events had seemed like simple bad luck. But now, to many in Salem Village, such incidents were evidence of witchcraft.

The First Accusations

But who was bewitching these unfortunate people? All of Salem Village wondered. At first the victims said nothing, but after repeated questioning, they began to name names: Sarah Good, Sarah Osborne, and Tituba. On February 29, Thomas Putnam, his brother Edward, and two others filed complaints against the three women, accusing them of hurting Betty Parris, Abigail Williams, Ann Putnam, Jr., and Elizabeth Hubbard.

The three women who were accused lived on the edges of society. Sarah Good, thirty-nine years old, had once been fairly prosperous but was now homeless, a beggar who went from house to house, seeking food and shelter. When she was refused, Good often cursed or insulted the homeowner. She was frequently absent from religious services because, she said, she had no proper clothes. Sarah Osborne, about forty-nine and ill, had lived a scandalous life. A widow, she kept her husband's land instead of giving it to his male heirs, as was the custom. She had also lived alone for several years with a male servant after her husband died and then married the servant. Tituba was a slave and a nonwhite; both of these qualities made her an automatic suspect in the eyes of the Puritans.

On March 1, the women were arrested and taken to Ingersoll's Tavern for a hearing (not a trial, because of the charter problem). So many people attended that the hearing was moved to the meetinghouse. The hearing would determine whether there was enough evidence to keep the women in jail until the legal situation could be straightened out. John Hathorne and Jonathan Corwin were the judges. While the accused women testified, the victims sat in the front of the crowded room, twisting their bodies and screaming in pain. Spectators tried in vain to comfort them. Deodat Lawson wrote of the "hideous screech and noise" that he heard, even though he was several blocks from the meetinghouse.[13]

Sarah Good was the first to be brought in. Her husband testified that his wife was either a witch or would soon become one and that she was "an enemy to all good."[14] She was asked why she had left the Parris house muttering under her breath and why Betty and Abigail had immediately fallen ill. She told the court that she had only been thanking the Lord for what the Parris family had given her child. Good was asked to recite a prayer, but she made several mistakes. To the Puritans, this failure was the typical behavior of a witch. Before she was led away, Sarah Good accused Sarah Osborne of hurting the girls.

Then Sarah Osborne came in. She was asked why she had not always attended Sunday services. She said that she was "frightened one time in her sleep" by "a thing like an Indian, all black, which did pinch her in her neck and pulled her by the back part of her head to the door of the house."[15] She said that the thing told her "that I should go no more to meeting but I said I would and did go the next Sabbath day."[16] The judges challenged her: Why had she not gone to meeting on other Sundays? Goody Osborne explained that she had been sick in bed.

Last to be questioned was Tituba. When she came into the room, the accusers went into fits. Tituba at first claimed to be ignorant of witchcraft, but the experience of being in the courtroom clearly affected her. At the end of the first day, she sat as if in a trance. Some observers wrote that Tituba was herself "very much afflicted [suffering]."[17] Eventually, Tituba broke down. She claimed that she had seen "a thing like a man" who told her to serve him, but she refused.[18] She said that Sarah Good and Sarah Osborne had indeed hurt the girls, and they had urged Tituba to join them in their witch-craft. However, Tituba had not agreed. Tituba said that the man had threatened to kill her if she would not serve him. She spoke of magical animals: a little yellow bird, a red cat, and a black cat. Finally, she claimed that she had ridden "upon a stick or pole and Good and Osborne behind me."[19]

The accused women were questioned for a total of five days. At one point Elizabeth Hubbard screamed. Although Sarah Good was not even in the room, Hubbard claimed that the specter (spirit) of Good had just jumped onto the table and threatened her. Samuel Sibley struck the table with his staff, so hard that the staff broke. No one laughed at this attempt to hit an invisible opponent. The next day Sibley claimed that he saw blood on Good's arm. He was sure that the blood resulted from his blow to Good's specter. Soon others in the courtroom said that they saw a strange, ghostly animal on the ground.

The judges ordered the three women to be jailed in Boston until their trial. The whole episode might have ended here, had the accusers recovered. However, most of them did not. Samuel Parris sent his daughter Betty to live with relatives, where she gradually improved. When she confessed to her experiments in fortune-telling, her fits stopped completely. But the others began to name more names. They moved beyond the outcasts into the ranks of mainstream Puritan society. In April, because of their growing importance, the hearings were moved to Salem Town. Such dignitaries as Deputy Governor Thomas Danforth and the Reverend Samuel Sewall attended.

The Circle of Witches Widens

Martha Cory was a clever woman. When the men came to arrest her, Martha Cory guessed why they had come, and she also guessed that the accusers would not be able to say what her specter was wearing when it supposedly appeared to them. The men did not think that Martha Cory was simply smart enough to figure out what they were going to do; they thought that she had used witchcraft to see the future.

The judges began Cory's hearing convinced that she was guilty. She protested that "I am an innocent person. I never had to do with witchcraft since I was born. I am a gospel women."[20] The girls screamed that she was "a gospel witch!"[21] They told the judges that Martha Cory had signed an agreement to give ten years to the devil. Six of those years had already passed. Giles Cory testified against his wife. He said that he found it difficult to pray when she was near. One of the spectators threw a shoe at Martha Cory and hit her on the head. A judge told her that if she expected to be forgiven, she must "first look for it in God's way by confession."[22]

The accusers also named Dorcas Good, four-year-old daughter of Sarah Good. Dorcas told stories to the magistrates about "a little snake that sucked on the lowest joint of her forefinger."[23] She said her mother had given her the snake.

John and Elizabeth Proctor were also arrested. The parents of five children, the youngest only three years old, the Proctors farmed land on the Ipswich Road. In 1666, John Proctor asked for a license to open a tavern. Many travelers stopped and asked him for food and drink, Proctor said in his license application. A practical man, he wanted to begin selling refreshment to these travelers instead of giving it away for free. The license was granted. When the witch trials began, John Proctor's no-nonsense attitude got him into trouble. He openly doubted that the accusers' suffering was real. One of his own servants, Mercy Warren, began to have fits, and he told her to work at her spinning wheel, fits or not. When John Indian accused the Proctors of witchcraft, John Proctor threatened to beat the foolishness out of him. He also said that the girls should be hanged. Elizabeth

Proctor's attitude was gentler than her husband's. She reminded the girls that "there is another judgment."[24] That is, the girls might fool the court, but they could not fool God.

Rebecca Nurse was also examined. During her hearing, the accusers watched her closely. When Nurse bent her head to one side, Elizabeth Hubbard snapped her own head into the same position. Abigail Williams cried, "Set up Goody Nurse's head . . . [or Hubbard's] neck will be broke."[25] The court officer straightened Nurse's head, and Elizabeth Hubbard relaxed. To many in the room, this incident proved that Rebecca Nurse had supernatural power that she used to hurt others.

More supposed proof was offered. Goodman Kenny said that once when Nurse had visited him, he was thrown into "an amazed condition."[26] Edward Putnam claimed that Rebecca Nurse had tortured his niece Ann. Goody Nurse answered, "I never afflicted [hurt] no child, no, never in my life."[27] She lifted up her arms and prayed, "Oh, Lord help me!" and the girls spread their arms as if forced.[28]

The magistrates questioned her. What did she think was the matter with the girls? Rebecca Nurse replied, "I cannot tell what to think . . . The Devil may appear in my shape."[29] Because the judges believed that the devil could not take the shape of an innocent person, Nurse's statement was seen as damaging to her case.

The Circle Widens Still More

Dorcas Good, Martha Cory, the Proctors, and Rebecca Nurse were all sent to jail, as were many others. The victims continued to have fits, and they continued to name names. Before the summer of 1692 had ended, Abigail Williams claimed that she had seen forty witches at a meeting. Susannah Post said there were two hundred witches there. Mary Toothaker reported that she had counted over three hundred.

A copy of Rebecca Nurse's arrest warrant for witchcraft is shown here.

The list of accused witches eventually grew to include people of high rank. Former minister George Burroughs was arrested in Maine. The wife of Nathaniel Cary, one of the wealthiest men in Cambridge, Massachusetts, was also arrested. One of the judges, Nathaniel Saltonstall, was accused, but the girls were told that they had been mistaken and the accusation was withdrawn.

The circle of victims widened also. As Cotton Mather wrote in his diary,

> The Devils . . . by the dreadful judgment of heaven, took a bodily possession of many people in Salem, and the adjacent [nearby] places: and the houses of the poor people began to be filled with the horrid cries of persons tormented by evil spirits.[30]

Communities outside Salem soon began to send for the witchcraft victims. The girls were invited to Andover to see if anyone there was a witch. The girls would be led into the presence of a suspected witch. If the girls fell into a fit, the suspect would go to jail. The townspeople must have wondered when and how the witchcraft would end.

Court of Oyer and Terminer

Into the middle of this crisis sailed William Phips, the new governor, on May 14, 1692. By authority of the long-awaited charter, Phips set up the Court of Oyer and Terminer almost before he left Boston Harbor. It was too late for Sarah Osborne, who died in jail on May 10, 1692. But the others readied themselves for the next part of the ordeal.

The first to be tried was Bridget Bishop. She had been

married three times, and it was rumored that she had
bewitched her husbands to death. Bishop was already a
scandal in the Puritan community because she wore clothes
that others found strange—a red silk vest, for example.
Witnesses testified that Bishop had caused pigs and chick-
ens to die and that she had overturned carts with her
supernatural powers.

*Rebecca Nurse is being accused of witchcraft. She, Dorcas Good,
Martha Cory, and the Proctors were all sent to jail, along with others.*

Samuel Shattuck also reported that Bishop had harmed his eldest child. Shattuck said that after Bishop visited once, his child became ill. Each additional visit made the child grow worse, although the child eventually recovered. About a year and a half after this episode, Shattuck heard about the witchcraft accusations. Suddenly the illness made sense to him. He remembered that Bishop had muttered some words as she left his house. He was now sure that these words were spells. With similar reasoning, William Stacy and Samuel Gray each testified that Bridget Bishop had caused the death of his child.

A builder testified that when he opened the wall in the basement of Bishop's house, he found pins and dolls. The court decided that these items were evidence of sorcery.

Bridget Bishop was found guilty and hanged on June 10, 1692. The other accused witches prepared for their trials, but nothing happened for several weeks. The delay was caused by an argument over evidence. Some of the Puritans, including Judge Nathaniel Saltonstall, were uneasy about accepting these accounts of witchcraft. Because specters were invisible to the court, there was no way to determine if the witnesses were lying or were themselves possessed by a devil. Saltonstall resigned in protest after Bishop's trial, but the other judges stayed on. However, Sir William Phips wrote to a group of ministers in Boston, asking for an opinion on spectral evidence.

The ministers' reply was mixed. No one should be convicted of witchcraft solely because of spectral evidence. The touch test was also unreliable, as was the prayer test, in which a suspected witch was asked to say the Lord's Prayer. The ministers stated that the court should be extremely careful in its dealings with people of good reputation. The ministers said that if too much weight were given to "things received only upon the devil's authority . . . a door [would be] opened for a long train of miserable consequences."[31] However, the last paragraph of the ministers' letter seemed to take back everything they had said previously. It urged the court to prosecute accused witches quickly and severely.

Reassured that they were acting quickly and severely, the Court of Oyer and Terminer met again. Soon it would be Rebecca Nurse's turn to face her accusers.

chapter four

THE ACCUSERS

NEW ENGLAND—"When I first arrived I found this province miserably harassed with a most horrible witchcraft or possession of devils some scalded with brimstone [devil's fire], some had pins stuck in their flesh, others hurried into the fire and water and some [were] dragged out of their houses and carried over the tops of trees and hills for many miles together."[1]

Who were the people who claimed to be "miserably harassed," as Sir William Phips put it? Why did they cry and tremble, or file complaints in a court of law? The first question was fairly easy to answer. Massachusetts was an educated, and organized community. Most Puritans could read and write, and some of them described the witch trials in their diaries, letters, and sermons. Although the official trial proceedings did not survive, many of the other court documents did. Today we can read the complaints, the written testimony prepared from witnesses, the orders of arrest and execution, and the records of pretrial hearings. The names of those who were "bewitched" and of those who took their accusations to the legal system are easy to determine.

Why they acted as they did is a more difficult question. The people of Salem Village undoubtedly believed in an invisible, dangerous world existing all around them. They were sure that the Devil was real and that he tempted human beings into his service by offering them magical powers. Moreover, many Puritans believed that they were the devil's special targets. Deodat Lawson declared that the Puritans, "those that would Devote themselves Intirely to his Service, are the Special Objects of SATAN'S Rage and Fury."[2] Cotton Mather said that Satan and his followers had hatched a "horrible plot" against Massachusetts, which, unless it were discovered and stopped, would "probably blow up and pull down all the churches in the country."[3]

Puritans of other communities also saw the world in the same way, as did the residents of Salem Village at other times, but this had never brought about a witchcraze. Clearly, unusual forces allowed the Puritans' beliefs to turn into a full-scale witch-hunt in 1692. In the past three centuries, historians, psychiatrists, lawyers, and many others interested in the Salem witchcraft trials have tried to understand the minds of the accusers. With few exceptions, the people directly involved never explained themselves. All we are left with is theory. Most historians believe that the bewitched and those who took their cases through the legal system had different reasons for their behavior.

The Bewitched

The daily life of a girl in seventeenth-century New England was very different from that of a boy. Gender roles in Puritan New England were strict. Boys worked in the fields or workshops with their fathers; they hunted and fished in the nearby woods and streams. Girls stayed home with their mothers, tending to the feeding, clothing, and child care of the family. Some writers of the time said that a good woman was never "a wanderer" but instead "a worker at home." The snail was used as a symbol of a good wife because it was a creature "that goes no further than it can carry its house on its head."[4]

Young Puritan women grew up hearing many sermons about their weak natures; they were also taught that females were especially tempted by the Devil. Many New England ministers owned or had read the *Malleus Maleficarum* (Latin for "Hammer of Witchcraft"), one of the basic textbooks for identifying and punishing witches. According to the *Malleus Maleficarum*, women were more likely to sin than men. The book also said that women were not as smart as men and had less physical strength. Therefore, the devil could tempt women by offering them riches and increased physical strength. The authors, two German priests, thanked God, "who has so far preserved the male sex from so great a crime."[5] The *Malleus Maleficarum* was a best-seller throughout Europe during the sixteenth and seventeenth centuries, second only to the Bible. Given its view of women, it is no surprise that the great majority of accused witches were female.

However, so too were the great majority of the bewitched women in Salem. Many historians see the actions of the bewitched girls as a search for power. As young people, and as females, their behavior was subject to many rules. They could not escape into the forest on a hunt, as

Young Puritan women grew up learning that females were especially tempted by the devil. Given this view of women, it is no surprise that the majority of those accused of witchcraft were women.

their brothers did. Like snails, they stayed in their houses all day, under the watchful eye of adults. Also, several of "the bewitched" were orphans living with relatives, and they were often treated as little more than servants. How exciting it must have been to shout in church, as one girl did, that the minister's planned sermon was too long. How free and powerful they must have felt running around the room, screaming and ignoring the adults who usually demanded instant obedience. Perhaps—without being aware of what they were doing—the girls suffered spells as a way of showing that they needed more freedom.

Many psychologists believe that at least some of the girls suffered from hysteria. Hysteria is a mental condition in which a person is aware of his or her actions but not able to control them. Sigmund Freud and Joseph Breuer, two important doctors who studied hysteria in the nineteenth century, thought that the condition arises from strong emotion that can not be expressed in normal life. The hysterical women that Freud and Breuer studied exhibited much of the same behavior as the bewitched girls of Salem Village. Other doctors have noted that people who feel powerless are more likely to experience hysteria. The young Puritan girls, in their strict society, would have been denied both emotional expression and power.[6]

Or perhaps the girls were aware of what they were doing. Some seventeenth-century observers suggested that the girls were performing tricks that they had carefully planned. Rebecca Nurse commented, "I do not think these suffer against their wills."[7] Robert Calef, a writer who

This petition was presented before the Court of Oyer and Terminer by Mary Esty, one of the many women accused as witches in Salem.

strongly criticized the witch-hunt, called the girls "the pretended afflicted."[8] The son of a famous Pilgrim, John Alden, Jr., of Plymouth, Massachusetts, wrote that the girls "played their juggling tricks, falling down, crying out, and staring into people's faces."[9] Alden was accused of being the head of all the witches in Boston.

Some evidence supports the theory of fakery. Daniel Elliot, "aged 27 years or there abouts,"[10] testified on March 28, 1692, that he was present when "one of the afflicted persons . . . cried out and said there's Goody Proctor."[11] William Rayment told the girl that "he believed she lied for he saw nothing."[12] Two other people were present, and they both agreed with Rayment. Instead of insisting that the specter was visible only to her, the girl admitted that there was nothing to see. Elliot testified that the girl said, "She did it for sport. They must have some sport."[13] In other words, she was playing a joke. In Andover, some afflicted girls named "a worthy gentleman of Boston" as a witch.[14] He immediately sued them for a thousand pounds—a huge sum of money. The girls never mentioned his name again.

There is other evidence of trickery. Rebecca Nurse's daughter saw Goody Bibber stick herself with a pin and claim that Goody Nurse's spirit had done it. Another time, one of the girls produced a piece of a knife and said that Goody Good's spirit stabbed her with it. A young man came forward and testified that it was his knife. The knife had broken while he was in the presence of the girl, and he saw her reach down and pocket a piece. In the presence of the court, the man put the two pieces of metal together. They fit perfectly. (The girl was scolded and reminded not to tell lies. However, the court accepted the rest of her testimony.)

Some fiction writers who used the events in Salem as the basis for plays and novels have suggested that at first the girls were simply trying to avoid punishment. The girls knew that they were in trouble for the fortune-telling games. Instead of admitting their guilt and accepting their fate, they began to have fits. The adults were soon so worried about witchcraft that they did not have time to discipline the young people. However, if this is indeed what happened in real life, once the adults went to court, the stakes were higher. To confess to a trick or to lying during a criminal trial was to confess to a crime. And if the trial was for a death-penalty crime—like witchcraft—lying was punishable by death. If the girls wanted to take back their testimony, they faced serious consequences.

Mary Warren, a servant in the Proctors' house, seems to have understood these consequences very well. Warren was one of the bewitched girls. She testified against Rebecca Nurse but balked when asked about others. She confessed that she and the other girls were lying. The other girls immediately began to scream that Mary Warren was afflicting them. Mary Warren was herself a witch, they claimed. Warren soon changed her story and rejoined the group.

Yet trickery does not explain every case. Some of the girls seem to have been suffering real pain. Some psychologists have pointed out that if you believe that you are bewitched, you will experience the effects that you expect to feel. That is, the power of witchcraft lies not in magic but in the belief in magical power. If the girls thought that the Devil had been raised in Massachusetts, as the Reverend Parris said, they would have expected to suffer. In looking for a reason for their suffering, they may have truly convinced themselves that the imaginary visions were real.

The Adult Accusers

In 1630, as a large group of Puritans was sailing to Massachusetts on the *Arabella*, John Winthrop told them that "[W]e must be knit together in this work as one man. We must delight in each other . . . labor and suffer together . . . as members of the same body."[15] Sixty-two years later, Winthrop's group was far from united, especially those Puritans living in Salem. Throughout New England, the Salem Villagers had gotten a reputation for quarreling. They fought with Salem Town over taxes and independence, and when they achieved some independence, they fought with one another over how to run their community. The colonial records are filled with lawsuits filed by the Farmers over boundary lines, inheritances, and salaries.

Some historians have analyzed these quarrels to see if they shed any light on the behavior of the adult accusers during the witch trials. The girls suffered fits, but it was the adults who filed the complaints and thus started the legal proceedings against their neighbors. While we will never know for sure, some of the quarrels in Salem seem to have bearing on the witch trials.

First of all, the village argued about whom to hire as its minister. Even when a minister was in place, the quarrels continued over whether to keep him. In 1692, the Salem Village church was divided into two groups—those who favored Parris and those who wanted him to resign. William Barker, an accused witch from the nearby community of Andover, said that Satan had picked Salem Village as a center of witchcraft "by reason of the people's being divided and their differing with the ministers."[16] He added that the plan was "to destroy Salem Village, and to begin at the minister's house, and to destroy the Church of God, and to set up Satan's Kingdom, and then all will be well."[17]

Parris himself was deeply involved in the witch trials; as Barker said, the outbreak of spells and strange behavior had started in the minister's house. Judging from the records of parish meetings and various letters and petitions, most of the adult accusers favored Samuel Parris. The majority of the accused Salem Village witches, on the other hand, opposed Parris and later signed a petition against him.

Another important conflict arose from the fact that in 1692 one way of life in Salem Village was ending and another was beginning. The earliest settlers of the Farms had owned large areas of land. By clearing the forest and by buying land from other settlers, the second generation of Farmers had increased their holdings. However, the third generation could not expect to do the same. Settled areas now surrounded Salem Village, so expansion into the forest was not a possibility. Also, as fathers died, they divided their land among their sons. A two-hundred-acre property supported a family nicely, but if it was split into two or three smaller farms, the sons could not expect to make a good living. The average Salem Village farm in the 1660s was nearly 250 acres, but by 1690, it was only 124 acres.[18]

Farmers watching their standard of living go down were living side by side with others who were watching their standard of living rise. The Village families with increasing riches often had strong ties to Salem Town, where there were many opportunities for business and trade. When the general court finally granted Salem Village full independence in 1752, it noted that most of the Town residents were "either merchants, traders, or mechanics."[19] The people in Salem Village, by contrast, were Farmers. The General Court observed that there were many difficulties "in the managing [of] their public affairs together."[20]

In the politics of Salem, these two groups were almost always on opposite sides. The Farmers tended to support the Reverend Parris. The people with ties to Salem Town generally opposed the minister. During the witchcraze, the Farmers frequently showed support for the trials, either by giving evidence or by bringing complaints. Members of the other group often signed petitions against the trials—or were on trial themselves.

Does this mean that Samuel Parris and the farming families tried to get rid of their enemies by means of a witch-hunt? Probably not. However, it may mean that the members of the pro-Parris group were more likely to think that the members of the other group were evil and practicing witchcraft. After all, everything in colonial Massachusetts was tied to religion. The Reverend Parris preached a sermon in September 1692 about choosing between God and the devil "Here are no neuters [neutrals]. Everyone is on one side or the other."[21] He might have been talking about Village politics, including the politics of the witch trials.

A Climate of Fear

Psychologists have noted that people who are afraid often lash out at their enemies. When real enemies are not available, imaginary enemies will do. Thus a climate of fear may have helped to bring about the witchcraze. Fear was widespread in New England during the late seventeenth century for several reasons.

First, the Puritans lived with the constant threat of attack by the American Indians who had once lived on the land the settlers now occupied. The American Indians objected to being forced from their homes by the newcomers. Besides losing their land, American Indians were also exposed to many new diseases brought by the colonists from Europe. The colonists had developed resistance to these infections, but the American Indians had not. Huge numbers grew sick and died. The American Indian population in New England, estimated at one hundred thousand in 1600, was down to twenty thousand by 1675.[22] Fighting for their lives, the survivors were determined to drive the Puritans away.

The American Indians constantly raided Puritan settlements and sometimes waged full-scale war. King Philip's War, which took place in 1675–1676, was particularly bloody. ("King Philip" was the name the colonists gave to Metacomet, the chief of the tribe fighting against them.) Nearly one fourth of the American Indian population of New

England died in the war. To make matters worse for the colonists, the American Indians were helped by the French, who were enemies of England and who could provide the American Indians with deadlier weapons such as muskets (guns) and gunpowder.

Puritan losses were also great, and the colonists heard many frightening stories about death and destruction at the hands of the attackers. George Burroughs once wrote to Boston for help in defending the settlement of York in what is now Maine. He described "Pillars of smoke, the raging of the merciless flames, the insults of the heathen [non-Christian] enemy, shouting, hooting, hacking [cutting up

In this painting by F. C. Yohn, one of the few men accused of being a witch is led off to the gallows.

bodies], and dragging away of 80 [colonists]."[23] In 1676, Mary Rowlandson described an attack at Lancaster, a town forty miles from Salem: "so many Christians lying in their blood . . . like a company of sheep torn by wolves, all of them stripped naked by a company of hell-hounds."[24] As the witch trials began, there were signs that a new war with the American Indians would soon erupt.

The bewitched girls may have been particularly afraid of the American Indians. Many of the girls had lost one or both parents in the conflict with American Indians. According to the beliefs of the Puritans, these girls had already suffered an attack by the devil; the Puritans saw the American Indians as agents of Satan. Cotton Mather described American Indians as "full of lying and Idleness, and sorcery [witchcraft]."[25] In one of his sermons he said that the devil had brought American Indians to New England in order to establish a kingdom there.[26]

Another fear was political. The new charter that Increase Mather brought from London in 1692 was worrisome to many Puritans. The colony would now be a royal province under the leadership of Governor William Phips. There was increased pressure to treat all religions equally. The Puritans' hold on the government and court system was threatened.

However, almost as soon as he set foot in New England, Sir William Phips left to defend the northern borders. Before he left, Phips authorized the Court of Oyer and Terminer to settle the witchcraft cases. All the magistrates Phips appointed were Puritans, and they, in turn, appointed Puritan juries. For a little while longer, the Puritans could carry on in their traditional ways.

Some Puritans worried that God was displeased with their community. Smallpox and influenza epidemics had swept the area in the 1670s and 1680s. A fire leveled Boston in 1679, and two comets had recently streaked across the sky. Many Puritans viewed these events as warnings of God's anger. The Puritans had come into existence because they wanted to purify their church. Now, many Puritans thought they had to purify their own community by casting out its witches.

chapter five

THE ACCUSED

WITCH HUNT—"Christ knows how many Devils there are in his Churches, and who they are."[1]

In Salem today you can stroll past any number of shop windows displaying souvenirs of the town's most famous period in history. But the only pictures we have of the defendants are pictures made of statistics. Two historians, John Demos and Carol Karlsen, created profiles from information they gathered in court, tax, and church records. One profile shows who was likely to be accused of witchcraft throughout New England during the entire colonial era. Another describes the typical witch in the Salem outbreak. (Of course, as with any generalization, it is important to remember that not everyone accused of witchcraft fit into these patterns.)

First of all, most witches were female. Of the 344 people accused of witchcraft in New England between 1620 and 1725, 267 were female. Half of the males were close relatives of the accused women and may have been considered suspects for that reason.[2] In Salem, about 75 percent of the people named as witches were female.[3]

In New England as a whole, those accused of being witches were more likely to be middle-aged. However, in Salem, an unusually high number of young people were jailed for witchcraft.[4] Almost all accused witches were married, both in Salem and throughout New England, but women who were widowed, separated, or divorced ran a greater risk of being accused.[5]

In colonial New England, women who had inherited property or who would soon inherit it were also more likely to be named as witches, as were those involved in a family conflict—a lawsuit over an inheritance, for example.[6] People who had already been charged with a crime such as theft or slander [telling lies that harm someone's reputation] were also more frequently accused.[7] Some of the Salem witches fit this pattern. Martha Cory, for example, was likely to inherit the estate of her elderly husband, Giles, simply because he was ten years older than she. In Salem, the families of several of the accused witches (such as sisters Rebecca Nurse, Mary Esty, and Sarah Cloyce) had been involved in lawsuits concerning the ownership of land. (Women were not allowed to sue.)

Judging from the court testimony, New Englanders often saw female witches as proud or discontented. Many challenged the established ideas of their society. In other words, they were more independent than the average Puritan female. Their independence, in Karlsen's view, put them at risk.[8] Some of the accused Salem witches (such as Sarah

Good and Martha Cory) were known for being outspoken and for having an unbending will.

Accepting the Will of God

An independent woman challenged the usual arrangement of Puritan society, which placed great emphasis on rank and order. Women were supposed to be obedient to men. One Puritan father gave this advice to his daughter as she prepared to marry, "Thy good husband here will be here with thee and comfort thee if thou submit and trust to him."[9] The poor were supposed to be obedient to the rich, and lay people were to obey ministers, and so forth. Because the Puritans believed that one's fate was determined before

Questioning authority was a sign of sin. Offenders suffered punishment by having their head and hands put in the pillory or their feet in the stocks. Some of the accused witches were known for being outspoken.

birth, any rebellion against the established order was a sin. In their view, holy people simply accepted the will of God. Cotton Mather, for example, wrote in his diary about a witchcraft case that occurred a few years before the events in Salem. He said that the witchcraft was a sign that people were "murmuring and repining [grieving] at the Providence of God" and were "discontented with their state . . . their poverty, or their misery."[10] Later, Mather commented on the "impudent" (disrespectful) accused witches in Salem who were already famous for their "discontented" behavior.[11] He wrote that when people were not happy with what God gave them, "the Devils do then invite them to an agreement."[12]

A Human Drama

But statistics tell only part of the story. We also have many individual portraits of the Salem defendants. These portraits are made of words drawn from the diaries, letters, and testimonies of the defendants and of those who knew them. Many small moments stand out in these documents and help us, more than three hundred years later, to remember that the defendants were real people caught in a terrible situation.

- Sarah Good leaped off her horse three times on the way to jail. Court documents noted that she tried to commit suicide.[13]

- Martha Cory hid her husband's saddle so that he could not ride to town. Cory went anyway, on foot, only to hear his own wife accused of witchcraft. He was named as a wizard (a male witch) a few weeks later.

- Little Dorcas Good was so young that the metal

bracelets used to chain her to the jail wall slipped off her wrists. The jailer had to make new, smaller bracelets just for her, and he billed her family for the work.

- George Burroughs was a graduate of Harvard, where he was probably the college's first star athlete. Burroughs was very proud of his strength and speed. During the witch-hunt his special ability was considered a sign of unnatural powers. Six people testified that Burroughs could hold a six-foot gun at arm's length with only one finger stuck in the barrel. They thought the devil must have helped Burroughs accomplish this feat.

- Elizabeth Cary was ill when she entered the court. Her husband, rich shipbuilder Nathaniel Cary, wrote that

> She was forced to stand with her arms stretched out. I did request that I might hold one of her hands, but it was denied me; then she desired me to wipe the tears from her eyes, and the sweat from her face, which I did; then she desired she might lean herself on me, saying she should faint.[14]

But John Hathorne, one of the judges, ordered Cary back to his seat. "She is strong enough to torment these girls," Hathorne said. "She should be strong enough to stand."[15]

- Samuel Wardwell tried to plead his innocence one last time as the hangman prepared the rope. However, Wardwell choked on smoke from the hangman's pipe. He could not say a word.[16]

Many Reactions

Some of the most interesting stories tell of the defendants' reactions to the witch-hunt. A few, like Sarah Good, were extremely angry. Just before she died, the Reverend Nicholas Noyes, a minister in Salem Town, asked her to confess. Sarah Good screamed, "I am no more a witch than you are a wizard, and if you take away my life, God will give you blood to drink."[17] Legend has it that Noyes died many years later with blood flowing out of his mouth. Bridget Bishop challenged the court also. She told the judge who asked her if she was a witch, "If I were such a person, you would know it."[18] This statement was seen as a threat. People thought that Bishop was saying that she would do something bad to the judge and then he would feel her power and know she was a witch.

Showing doubt about the bewitched or the legal process often brought disaster. John Proctor said that the girls should "be had to the Whipping post."[19] Proctor's cure for the bewitched was simple. "Hang them, hang them," he cried.[20] The next day the girls cried out against Proctor's wife. John Proctor was soon named as a wizard. Goody Cloyce walked out of the service on the Sunday after her sister Rebecca Nurse was arrested. Reverend Parris had chosen to preach a sermon based on the Bible verse, "Have not I chosen you twelve, and one of you is a Devil."[21] Deodat Lawson noted that Cloyce "flung the door after her violently."[22] A few days later the girls said they saw Goody Cloyce in a field with a group of witches, performing a satanic ceremony. Soon Sarah Cloyce was named as a witch. John Willard, a constable (an officer of the law), was arrested for witchcraft after he refused to arrest anyone else on that charge. Similarly, Dudley Bradstreet, a justice of the peace in Andover, refused to sign any more arrest warrants after over thirty people had been jailed. He and his wife were quickly accused.

Some defendants tried to prove their innocence, right to the end. George Burroughs said the Lord's Prayer just before he was hanged.[23] Tradition held that the devil would not let his followers recite the prayer correctly. In fact, when one defendant said "hollowed be Thy name" instead of "hallowed," the mistake was seen as proof of her guilt.[24] At Burroughs' execution, the crowd began to turn in his favor when he finished without error. However, Cotton Mather told them that the devil had often been transformed (changed) "into an angel of light."[25] So Burroughs' perfect prayer was considered just another of the devil's tricks.

Other defendants pleaded for mercy for themselves and others. Mary Esty and her sister Sarah Cloyce asked the court to advise them during the trial since neither knew anything about the law. The court refused. Esty wrote a gentle letter to the court when she was convicted. Esty's letter is full of concern for the community of Salem. "I petition to your honors not for my own life, for I know I must die," she said. Then she asked that the court reconsider its methods "that no more innocent blood be shed." Knowing that she herself was innocent and that the girls were lying in her case, Esty said that the others "going the same way [as] myself" (that is, accused of witchcraft) must also be innocent.[26] Goody Esty asked that the girls be questioned separately; she was sure their stories would not match and their lies would be revealed. Her petition was ignored.

Some accused witches decided that they would never get

a fair trial and that escape was the only answer. Nathaniel Cary, probably with the help of bribes, broke into the jail and rescued his wife. The two fled to Rhode Island and then to New York, where the governor welcomed them. Eventually New York City, which was not a Puritan settlement, became the home of a small band of refugees from the witch-hunt. John Alden was another accused witch who escaped, though he was eventually recaptured.

Confession

In England, most of the people who confessed to the crime of witchcraft were put to death. However, in Salem the opposite was true. Those who maintained their innocence were more likely to die than those who pled guilty and asked forgiveness for their crime.

The first to confess was Tituba. Even before her hearing, Tituba was pressured by Samuel Parris to admit that she was a witch. Historian Elaine Breslaw has compared Tituba's statements to the beliefs of Indians from the coast of South America. She identified many elements in Tituba's story that match the folklore of magic in that region. For example, the Arawak tribe believes in kenaimas—real people who can cause sickness or evil for others. Kenaimas are often described as hairy. They can change shapes or inhabit animals, particularly birds. In her confession, Tituba told the judges about "an other thing hairy it goes upright like a man" and "a yellow bird" belonging to the creature.[27]

In Breslaw's view, Tituba matched ideas from her Indian legends to the Puritans' ideas about witchcraft. She created a story to satisfy the judges, hoping that if they believed she had practiced witchcraft and was now repenting, they might spare her life. If this really was Tituba's strategy, it was a good one. Tituba did survive the witch-hunt, although she remained in jail for many months.

Tituba may also have confessed because she believed that nothing else would satisfy the judges. That is why Sarah Churchill made her statement. Churchill went to see Sarah Ingersoll, the innkeeper's daughter, crying and wringing her hands. Ingersoll wrote that Churchill falsely admitted to signing the devil's book. According to Ingersoll, Churchill said, "if she told Mr. Noyes but once she had set her hand to the book, he would believe her; but, if she told the truth, and said she had not set her hand to the book a hundred times, he would not believe her."[28]

The judges were not the only ones who pressed for confession.

> Goodwife Tyler of Andover knew she was innocent when she was arrested and she did think that nothing could have made her confess . . . She said that when she was brought to Salem her brother Bridges rode with her and that all along the way from Andover to Salem her brother kept telling her that she must . . . be a witch, since the afflicted accused her . . . [and he kept] urging her to confess herself a witch.[29]

Threatened with hanging, Tyler confessed, but later she said that her confession was a lie.

Some of the confessions were obtained by torture. Increase Mather investigated this issue, visiting jails and questioning those who had confessed. He reported that "for above eighteen hours . . . [the] most violent . . . methods had been used" on some of the prisoners.[30] One was "tying neck and heels," a traditional English practice in which the prisoner's body was forced into a hoop, the neck tied to the ankles. The two teenage sons of Martha Carrier confessed to witchcraft and gave evidence against their mother after experiencing this torture. William Proctor refused to testify against his parents, even though he was tied for more than a day and blood "gushed out at his nose."[31]

Under torture, Margaret Jacobs confessed that she had practiced witchcraft. She gave evidence against her grandfather, George Jacobs, and against George Burroughs. When her grandfather was sentenced to death and she was spared, Margaret Jacobs took back her confession. Jacobs wrote,

> The Lord above knows I knew nothing, in the least measure, how or who afflicted them . . . they told me if I would not confess, I should be put down into the dungeon and would be hanged, but if I would confess, I should have my life . . . to save my life made me make the confession I did, which confession, may it please the honoured court, is altogether false and untrue.[32]

The court, nevertheless, carried out her grandfather's death sentence. Before he died, George Jacobs declared, "Burn me or hang me, I will stand in the truth of Christ, I know nothing of it."[33] Margaret Jacobs was allowed to visit her grandfather and George Burroughs to ask their forgiveness.

The Guilty

Some people may have confessed because they really were trying to practice witchcraft and they had convinced themselves that they had signed the devil's book. (Of course, it is impossible to know which confessions were sincere.) Some of the people who confessed explained what the witches had been promised in return for their service to Satan. Many of the rewards were small: "new clothes," "a piece of money," "a pair of French fall shoes."[34] Other promised—and imagined—rewards were more signigicant. Mary Toothaker explained,

> Last May I was greatly depressed, and I was troubled with fear about the Indians. I used often to dream of fighting with them. . . . The Devil appeared to me in the shape of a tawny man and promised to keep me from the Indians. . . . He promised, if I would serve him, I should be safe from the Indians.[35]

(Mary Toothaker and her nine-year-old daughter were in prison when the Indians burned their house down. Three years later, the Indians killed her and carried away her daughter, who was never seen again.)

One person who *did not* confess was Rebecca Nurse. She was bewildered by her arrest, but she was sure she would be found innocent. So when the jury returned to the courtroom for the second time, with a second verdict, Rebecca Nurse was ready.

chapter six

THE VERDICT

COURTROOM—"I believe, there never was a poor Plantation, more pursued by the . . . [anger] of the Devil, than our poor New-England."[1]

As the jury filed in, each person in the crowd must have been trying to answer Chief Justice Stoughton's question. Why had Rebecca Nurse called a confessed witch "one of us"? And why, when the jury asked her to explain, did she say nothing? Thomas Fisk, the head of the jury, announced the verdict. This time, the jury found Rebecca Nurse guilty of witchcraft. The bewitched girls in the front of the courtroom went wild, and a howl rose from the street outside. (By now so many people claimed to be under a spell that they could not all fit in one room.) Dazed, Goodwife Nurse heard Chief Justice Stoughton sentence her to death by hanging. As Nurse was led away, Stoughton turned his attention to the others who stood trial that day: Sarah Good, Susannah

Martin, Elizabeth Howe, and Sarah Wild. They all received death sentences also.

Now it was time for Rebecca Nurse to suffer another type of death sentence. Shortly after her trial, Nurse was carried in a chair to the Salem Town meetinghouse. Though she usually attended services in Salem Village near her home, she was officially still part of the Salem Town church. Goodwife Nurse was so weak that she could not even stand up when Nicholas Noyes, minister of Salem Town, called for a vote. Should this convicted witch be thrown out of the church?

Everyone voted yes. In Puritan eyes, a witch could not be a visible saint, so Rebecca Nurse was now a stranger to everything holy. The congregation knew that her fate was clear—when Rebecca Nurse's life ended in the hangman's noose, her soul was bound for hell.

But Nurse was not ready to give up. Now that the trial was over, Rebecca Nurse recovered her senses enough to understand her situation. She wrote a letter to the court in which she explained her comment. Nurse stated that when she said that Deliverance Hobbs was "one of us," she meant only that Hobbs was also a prisoner. Rebecca Nurse already knew that Deliverance Hobbs had been accused of witchcraft and jailed. However, Nurse did not know that Hobbs had confessed and had begun to give evidence against others. As to her silence in the courtroom, Rebecca Nurse explained that she was "something hard of hearing and full of grief."[2] She had not tried to avoid the jury's question; she simply had not heard it.

Rebecca Nurse's letter did not impress William Stoughton. However, either her reputation in the community or the pleas of those who loved her did sway Governor Phips. He granted her a reprieve; that is, he said that her sentence should not be carried out. But it was widely reported that at the very moment Phips signed the reprieve, the girls screamed out with even greater force. Goody Nurse was torturing them, they claimed. Faced with this report and with the demands of their relatives, Governor Phips gave in. He took back the reprieve and cleared the way for Rebecca Nurse's death by hanging.

Gallows Hill

Today, climbing Gallows Hill—probably a spot north of Salem Town where a sturdy oak tree once stood—is easy. The road is paved and we have automobiles. But in the seventeenth century, the Puritans went up Gallows Hill on foot or in horse-drawn carts. The road was full of ruts and stones, and after a rainstorm, it was a sea of mud. On the way to one hanging, the cart holding the condemned witches got stuck. The bewitched girls, who attended every hanging, cried out that the devil was holding the cart, trying to save his followers. The villagers freed the cart from the mud and continued on their way up the hill.

Many in Salem followed; large crowds, loudly mocking the condemned prisoners, witnessed the executions. Before the death sentence was carried out, each witch was allowed to speak to the crowd. According to eyewitnesses, all of the unfortunate Puritans scheduled to die on July 19, 1692, insisted that they were innocent, right to the end. Rebecca Nurse prayed to God for a miracle that would prove her innocence. She also asked God to forgive those who had wronged her. Then she died.

The Puritans believed that executed witches did not deserve a religious burial. The bodies were simply pushed into cracks or holes and covered with a thin layer of dirt. Tradition says that Rebecca Nurse's family could not accept such a fate. The story is that they returned to Gallows Hill late that night, removed her body, and buried it properly. Today, no one knows exactly where the remains of Rebecca Nurse lie. However, there is a monument to her in a small burial ground near the Nurse homestead. The monument is very close to the site of Samuel Parris's parsonage, where the witchcraze began.

More Hangings

More trials, more death sentences, and more hangings quickly followed the July 19, 1692, executions. The Proctors were found guilty, as were George Burroughs, George Jacobs, Martha Carrier, and Constable John Willard. This group was scheduled for execution on August 19. John Proctor asked for more time in order to prepare his soul for death, but he was refused. Elizabeth Proctor was spared, for the time being, because she was expecting a baby. The rest were hanged.

On September 9, six more accused witches were sentenced to death, and on September 17, nine more received the same verdict. One of the condemned was Martha Cory.

Like Rebecca Nurse, Martha Cory was also expelled from her church before the hanging. Her husband, Giles Cory, was not hanged with his wife, but he did not escape death. When he was brought before the court, he was asked if he pleaded guilty or innocent. Old Giles Cory would not say a word. Perhaps he was angry at the whole proceeding, or perhaps he thought that his silence would save him. Legally, the trial could not proceed until an official plea had been entered

This monument to Rebecca Nurse stands in Danvers, Massachusetts, as a reminder of a time when hysteria and confusion prevailed.

in the record. So the court officers took Cory to a field and stretched him out on the ground. They placed some heavy rocks on his chest. Based on an old English method of torture, the idea was to "press" the words out of him. But Giles Cory was a stubborn man. For two days, the judges asked him to plead and piled more stones on top of him when he refused. Finally, there was so much weight on his chest that Giles Cory could not breathe. He never entered a plea, though tradition says that he did say one thing, over and over: "More weight."[3]

Lost Property, Lost Lives

In addition to those who were executed, some grew sick and died in prison. Chained to a post or to the wall, in dark, dirty rooms without any way to clean themselves or to rest comfortably, the accused witches suffered physically as well

as mentally. Sarah Osborne died in prison, as did three other adults and the newborn baby of Sarah Good. Little Dorcas Good, described as healthy and "well-looking" when she was arrested, was not the same when she was released.[4] Years later her father said that his "child of about four

The Reverend George Burroughs stands accused of witchcraft. He was eventually tried, hung, and buried beneath the gallows.

or five years old was in prison seven or eight months and being chain'd in the dungeon was . . . hardly used [treated badly] and terrifyed."[5] William Good added that his daughter would always have to depend on the charity of others because "she hath ever since . . . little or no reason [sanity] to govern herself."[6] In other words, prison drove Dorcas Good insane. The mother of a fourteen-year-old girl who spent nine months in jail on a charge of witchcraft said that "imprisonment was more to our damage than I can think of, know, or can speak."[7]

The families of the executed witches lost more than their loved ones. According to Massachusetts law, the property of convicted witches had to be turned over to the government. The state showed no mercy to a witch family—not even to the youngest children.

The Proctors are a good example. After John and Elizabeth Proctor were found guilty, the sheriff went to their farm. He took "all the goods, provisions [food] and cattle . . . threw out the beer . . . emptied a pot of broth . . . and left nothing in the house for the support of the children."[8] How cruel a punishment this was in a time when every household supplied itself with the necessities of life. There were no stores for the Proctor children to turn to, no help except for the charity of their neighbors.

But the law was clear. All the possessions of a convicted witch or wizard, except for land, had to be turned over to the state. So when George Jacobs' wife asked for his wedding ring, she was told that she would have to buy it back from the sheriff. Since all the property was in her husband's name, she also had to purchase the contents of her own house. And when George Burroughs died wearing a fine suit, the sheriff put some old rags on the body and sold the suit.

The Turning Point

On September 22, eight more people were hanged. These deaths marked the turning point of the Salem witch trials. While over a hundred colonists remained in jail, no more were executed. The episode was nearing its end, and not a moment too soon. If the Salem witch trials had continued, the entire colony might have failed. The community was so wrapped up in the supernatural that they neglected the real things they had to do to ensure their physical survival. The accused, of course, could not work because they were in jail. Their relatives and supporters were busy writing petitions, attending trials, and visiting the prison. Neither did the afflicted girls and their relatives have time for the usual chores. The town officials were also occupied with witch duties. A marshal in Salem, for example, petitioned the government for help. He had been so busy arresting people, he said, that he did not have enough food to get through the winter. He had had no time for his "poor farm."[9]

Perhaps, as the summer of 1692 ended, the threat of the approaching winter made people think more about natural, rather than supernatural things. Perhaps the girls had reached too high. Perhaps the community had simply seen enough arrests, enough death.

Or perhaps Andover had shown them that the witchcraze

could end. The afflicted girls had been visiting that town, identifying witches and undergoing their usual fits. Forty citizens of Andover had been jailed on charges of witchcraft before the judge refused to sign any more arrest warrants. Soon a petition went from Andover to the General Court. In the petition the witchcraft victims were called "distempered persons"(mentally ill). How could the community listen to their testimony, the people of Andover asked. Their petition stated, "We know no one who can think himself safe if the accusations of children and others who are under diabolical [devilish] influence shall be received against persons of good fame."[10] The tide of public opinion was beginning to turn against the girls. During a visit to the town of Gloucester, they passed an old woman and began to scream that she was a witch and was tormenting them. No one paid any attention to the girls, and their fits ended. Eventually the girls got up and walked away.

Cases of Conscience

Another important factor in ending the witchcraze was a sermon preached by Increase Mather on October 3, 1692. It was later published under the title "Cases of Conscience Concerning Evil Spirits Personating [pretending to be] Men." In his sermon, Increase Mather strongly disapproved of spectral evidence and the touch test. Anyone who used these tests, he explained, was relying on the devil's own methods to prove witchcraft. He disagreed with a statement that one of the judges, John Hathorne, had made during the hearing for George Jacobs. When Jacobs claimed, "The

Devil can take any [person's] likeness," Hathorne had replied, "Not without their consent."[11] Increase Mather made his position extremely clear. "It were better," he said, "that ten suspected witches should escape, than one innocent person should be condemned."[12] Fourteen other ministers signed Mather's sermon, giving their approval to his ideas.

The General Court could not ignore such a forceful publication. In late October it called for a meeting of ministers "that may be led in the right way as to the witchcraft."[13] The right way was soon clear. After more than twenty deaths, the Court of Oyer and Terminer was dismissed. In its place a new Superior Court was established. William Stoughton would again be Chief Justice. However, now he had to work from new rules of evidence. Specifically, Governor Phips told him that spectral evidence was no longer acceptable. Since the remaining cases were all based on this type of evidence, almost all the witches who had not yet been tried were soon declared not guilty. Governor Phips granted reprieves to the rest, and in May, 1693 he ordered all accused witches still in jail to be released.

"The Guilt of Innocent Blood"[14]

Yet even now the ordeal was not over for many of the previously imprisoned Puritans. They were billed for their lodging and food in the jail, and even for their chains. Edward and Sarah Bishop, parents of twelve children, were in prison for thirty-seven weeks. They were charged ten shillings a week each, and five pounds extra for expenses. This sum would be large for any Puritan family, even in normal times. But paying such a bill after nine months in prison was even more difficult. The sheriff had taken most of their farm animals and household goods, and they had not harvested any crops since the previous year. No one was released from jail until the account was settled. Tituba, for example, owed seven pounds for her eight months in jail, but as a slave, she had no money. The Reverend Parris did not want to pay her bill; in his view, she had started the trouble with her fortune-telling. Finally, after an extra year in jail, someone bought Tituba and paid her debts. She was free from jail, but she was still a slave in someone else's house.[15]

The record is unclear, but it is likely that her husband, John Indian, was sold with her, because the Puritans believed that it was wrong to break up a married couple. John Indian had never gone to jail; in fact, he was one of the bewitched. Some historians believe that John Indian knew that as a nonwhite and a slave, he was an easy target. They think that he may have accused others to avoid being named as a wizard himself. (Interestingly, the jury refused to convict Tituba of witchcraft, even though she confessed to the crime. They brought back a verdict of "ignoramus." That is, they said that they were ignorant about her guilt or innocence and could not make a decision.)

Slowly, the colony returned to normal life. The girls calmed down, and many of them married and began to raise families. Or, as the Reverend John Hale put it, "the Lord chained up Satan, that the afflicted grew presently well."[16] The Reverend Parris began another salary fight with his congregation; a few years later, he was forced out of his job as minister to Salem Village. Thomas Putnam and his wife, Ann, who made so many of the witchcraft complaints, died soon after.

Petitions for Justice

But the families of the accused witches could not forget. They had begun to petition the General Court for justice even before the trials were over. At first they asked for simple things: Could their relatives be freed on bail so that they could await their trials in their own homes? Later they challenged the trials themselves, claiming that their relatives were not given a fair hearing. They wanted the verdicts to be overturned and their relatives' reputations cleared. They also wanted the colony to pay damages for the harm they had suffered during the witch trials. In 1709, Isaac Esty, husband of the executed Mary Esty, wrote that her estate had been "damnified by reason of such hellish molestation."[17] Benjamin Proctor wanted money from the state because he had "helped bring up all my father's children by all his wives."[18] The five children of George Burroughs also sued because of their father's suffering and death as a convicted wizard. In 1710, the General Court passed a law clearing the names of the convicted witches whose relatives had petitioned. A year later, the state settled many of the financial claims.

In 1950, descendants of other executed witches asked for an official pardon. The Massachusetts government told them that they could not grant a pardon because the prosecutions had taken place while Massachusetts was still part of

England. Only the British government could grant a pardon for convictions from the colonial era. However, the British courts said that they no longer had any power in Massachusetts and therefore could do nothing. Finally, in 1957, the state of Massachusetts passed a resolve removing the "guilt and shame" from descendants of the victims.

Apologies

Not all the efforts to put things right involved money. Many of the people who had played major roles in the witch-craze apologized to their victims, although sometimes the apologies arrived years later. In November 1694, the Reverend Samuel Parris stated, "I do heartily, fervently, and humbly beseech pardon . . . of all my mistakes and trespasses in so weighty a matter."[19] A few years later another minister, John Hale, wrote that

> I have had a deep sen[s]e of the sad consequence of mistakes in matters Capital [death penalty cases] . . . such was the darkness of that day, the tortures and lamentations [groans] of the afflicted . . . that we walked in the clouds, and could not see our way.[20]

Samuel Sewall announced in 1697 that he accepted "blame and shame" for his role as judge.[21]

One of the most detailed apologies came from Ann Putnam, Jr., who was usually the first of the afflicted girls to accuse a new witch. Putnam, who never married, applied for full membership in the Salem Village church when she was twenty-six years old. She told the congregation that "it was a great delusion [trick] of Satan that deceived me in that sad time, whereby I justly fear I have . . . [played a role], with others, though ignorantly and unwittingly [without knowing], to bring upon myself and this land the guilt of innocent blood."[22] Putnam was admitted to the church; she died nine years later at the age of thirty-seven.

The twelve members of the jury that convicted Rebecca Nurse also asked for pardon, saying that they felt "the guilt of innocent blood."[23] They said that "we would none of us do such things again on such grounds for the whole world."[24] Twenty years after her death, Rebecca Nurse received the apology that would probably have meant the most to her. On March 2, 1712, the First Church of Salem admitted that it had made a mistake in casting her out of the church. The First Church said that it was canceling its previous vote on Nurse, "that it may no longer be a reproach to [stain on] her memory and an occasion of grief to her children."[25] Rebecca Nurse was once more a visible saint.

chapter seven

THE AFTERMATH

SALEM VILLAGE—"And among Satans Mysteries . . . this of Witchcraft is one of the most difficult to be searched out by the Sons of men."[1]

Despite all of the apologies, the Puritans continued to believe in the existence of witches. Many viewed the trials of 1692 as wrong, but only because innocent people had been accused and tried on the basis of spectral evidence. The Reverend John Hale expressed a common opinion. He stated that it would be a mistake to ignore witchcraft crimes just because the trials of 1692 had gone astray. He cautioned the Puritans that there were still persons who "by the Devil's aid discover secrets, or do work wonders"[2] and such persons should be arrested and tried. The Reverend John Higginson agreed and added that the Puritans should try to find out how to catch witches in such a way that "innocent persons may be preserved, and none but the guilty may suffer."[3]

Witchcraft trials that

took place in Massachusetts after 1692 followed a new law written by the General Court. Those convicted of using magic to find treasure or to create love potions would be sentenced to a year in jail. Anyone using witchcraft to harm another human being would still receive the death penalty. In 1703, the Massachusetts House of Representatives passed a law saying that spectral evidence would no longer be allowed in any trial. It added a provision stating that the bad reputations of people convicted of witchcraft because of spectral evidence should "in some measure be rolled away."[4] In 1736, England and Scotland repealed all laws against witchcraft. Massachusetts, still a British colony, did the same. Though witchcraft was no longer a formal crime, it was still looked down on, even after the colonies gained their independence from Britain. In fact, in July 1787, while delegates in Philadelphia were busy writing the Constitution of the United States, a suspected witch was attacked by a mob a few streets away. The victim died of her injuries.

The Constitution that the founders were writing did not mention religion. However, almost as soon as the Constitution went into effect, Americans realized that it was incomplete. The Bill of Rights, made up of ten amendments or changes, was added. The First Amendment ordered that "Congress shall make no law respecting an establishment of religion, or prohibiting the free exercise thereof."[5]

Were the authors of the Bill of Rights thinking of Salem's mixture of government and religion when they wrote that amendment? Probably not. However, they may have been reacting to abuses of power by established religions during the colonial period. As Supreme Court Justice Hugo Black wrote in 1947 in *Everson v. Board of Education*, an important case about freedom of religion, the nation's founders knew that problems arose when only one religion was recognized. Black said that "A large proportion of the early settlers of this country came here from Europe to escape . . . laws which . . . [forced] them to support and attend government favored churches."[6] However, Black added, the settlers often repeated the same practices they had objected to in Europe. Often colonists had to pay taxes to support government-approved churches "whose ministers preached . . . sermons designed to strengthen . . . the established faith by . . . [creating] a burning hatred against dissenters [those who disagreed]."[7] Black felt that these practices came to "shock the freedom-loving colonials" and eventually led to the First Amendment.[8]

The First Amendment guarantees what Thomas Jefferson called "a wall of separation between church and state."[9] The Salem trials, powered by a mix of religious beliefs and law, could not take place under our current system of government. In the legal system we now enjoy, juries are made up of people with differing views of the world—not one view, as the Puritan juries were. Defendants on trial now are considered innocent until proven guilty. The prosecutors must present evidence that clearly shows guilt beyond a reasonable doubt. Judges are supposed to be fair to both sides, and lawyers represent the accused. As was true of all English courts of the period, the defendants in Salem were allowed none of these rights.

Modern Witch-Hunts

The Puritans of Salem created an important pattern of behavior. Americans, even centuries later, often refer to this pattern—the witch-hunt—when they interpret current events. The Salem witch trials can never be repeated—at least not in exactly the same way. Yet in modern America people may also be "tried" in the media or in the political arena. These are areas where we may see a modern witch-hunt.

In fact, the witch-hunt is so much a part of our national memory that the phrase has become part of the American vocabulary. It is used when a wave of accusations and trials for some offense breaks out. These days, the offense is usually not witchcraft, but rather something that many people find frightening, such as unpopular political beliefs. During a modern witch-hunt, large groups of people are questioned and urged to confess to their crimes. Some may be offered pardons if they name other people involved in the wrongdoing and if they give evidence against their former friends and neighbors. Even without a trial, reputations and careers may be ruined.

Like Salem's, the witch-hunts of modern times often end with a backlash. The media start to question the motives of the court. The evidence begins to appear flimsy or faked, and some of those who confess say that they did so only to save themselves. Finally, society begins to wonder how so many people lost their usual good sense. The witch-hunt dies down, and everyone breathes a sigh of relief—until the next time.

The anti-Communist trend in the United States in the 1950s is a good example of a modern witch-hunt. As World War II ended, the Union of Soviet Socialist Republics (USSR), a communist nation, was locked in the Cold War with the United States. Many countries in Eastern Europe fell under Communist rule, and a large number of Americans believed that the Communists' long-range plan was to take over the United States. Membership in the Communist party in the United States was legal, but greatly criticized. In 1950, Senator Joseph McCarthy of Wisconsin made a speech in Wheeling, West Virginia. He said that "the world is split into two . . . armed camps,"[10] those who favored democracy and the United States and those who favored communism and the Soviet Union. Waving a piece of paper, McCarthy said, "I have in my hand 57 cases of individuals who would appear to be either card carrying members or certainly loyal to the Communist party."[11] These fifty-seven people, McCarthy claimed, worked in the American government. Another time he claimed to have a list of 205 members of the Communist Party who were "working and shaping policy in the State Department."[12] In fact, McCarthy had no lists at all.

McCarthy's speech added to the fear of communism that was already widespread in the United States. Americans from all across the country were summoned to Washington and questioned: "Are you now or have you ever been a member of the Communist Party?" As in the Salem witch trials, just the fact that someone was named was proof of guilt in many people's eyes. Those questioned were urged to confess and to name others who supposedly sympathized with Communist ideas.

Some of those accused of being Communist sympathizers probably were, just as a couple of the accused Salem witches probably were trying to practice magic. However, as in Salem, the circle of accusations grew wider and wider. At one point, even the Girls Scouts were suspected of having Communist ideas.

In 1953, playwright Arthur Miller wrote a drama entitled *The Crucible*. Set in seventeenth-century Salem, Miller created fictional characters loosely based on the historical record. In *The Crucible*, John and Elizabeth Proctor, Abigail Williams, and others appear. The fictional John Proctor is urged to confess to save his life, just as the Salem witches— and the accused Communists—were. Proctor refuses to confess to something he did not do, and he is hanged. Miller's play was set in the time of the first witch-hunt, but it was clearly intended to make the audience think about the anti-Communist witch-hunt they were then living through.

As in Salem, the backlash against Joseph McCarthy and anti-Communist investigations eventually grew strong enough to end the episode. However, for years afterward, many of those who had been questioned, particularly people from the entertainment industry, were unable to find work. They were blacklisted; that is, no one would employ them for fear of appearing sympathetic toward Communists.

If she could somehow return to Massachusetts today, Rebecca Nurse might go to the town of Danvers, a few miles from Salem. Danvers is the name that Salem Village took when it became independent of Salem Town in 1752. Visitors to Danvers can stop in at the Nurse homestead, a colonial building on the farm that once belonged to Goody Nurse and her family. In the late afternoon, after the cars have left and the last tours have ended, it is possible to stand on Rebecca Nurse's property and enjoy a view very like the one that met her eyes in 1692. It is easy to imagine the old Puritan woman standing quietly on her farm, thinking about the afflicted girls and wondering what was going on in her little village.

More than three hundred years later, we wonder also.

The Rebecca Nurse Homestead in Danvers, Massachusetts, reminds us of the many women who died during a period in our history when the accused were not afforded the same rights that we enjoy today.

Questions for Discussion

1. Imagine that you live in Salem in 1692, and your neighbor is arrested for witchcraft. You think that your neighbor is innocent. What would you do?

2. Given their beliefs, should the Puritans have allowed spectral evidence in the trials?

3. The defendants in Salem were not allowed to have a defense attorney. Unlike modern defendants, they also were not considered "innocent until proven guilty." How would the trials have been different if the Puritans had allowed these two rights?

4. What are some of the advantages and disadvantages of a community in which everyone shares the same goals and beliefs?

5. Both in Europe and in seventeenth-century Massachusetts, most of the people tried for witchcraft were female. Why do you think that more women than men were accused?

6. If you were giving advice to the accused witches, what would you say? How would you suggest that they defend themselves?

7. Why do you think that witch-hunts are more likely to occur during periods of social change?

8. A few of the accused witches in Salem may actually have tried to practice magic. Should the attempt to practice magic be a crime?

9. Think about the images of witches in today's media (*Sabrina the Teenage Witch, The Wizard of Oz*). How are today's images different from the images of witches in Puritan times? What do the differences tell you about each era?

10. Have you ever heard a rumor or a false accusation spread throughout your community, your school, or throughout the media? Do people today tend to believe the rumors they hear?

Chapter Notes

Author's Note on Sources:

The original records of the Salem Witch Trials are handwritten, with many variations in spelling and punctuation. In this book, some of the spelling and grammar has been changed to make the quotation more readable. Changes in quotes are indicated within brackets. A little of the original has been left in order to give the reader the flavor of the original document. The witchcraft papers were typewritten during the 1930s. Historians Paul Boyer and Stephen Nissenbaum published the papers in *Salem-Village Witchcraft: A Documentary Record of Local Conflict in Colonial New England* (Belmont, Calif.: Wadsworth Publishing Co., 1972). Most of the books listed in the "Chapter Notes" quote from one of those two sources in their work.

Chapter 1. Witches on Trial

1. John Winthrop, "A Model of Christian Charity," Winthrop Papers (Boston: The Massachusetts Historical Society, 1931) vol. 11, p. 295.

2. *Deuteronomy*, King James Version, 18:10–11.

3. Enders A. Robinson, *The Devil Discovered* (New York: Hippocrene, 1991), pp. 12–13.

4. Marian L. Starkey, *The Devil in Massachusetts* (New York: Doubleday, 1949), p. 81.

5. Frances Hill, *A Delusion of Satan* (New York: Doubleday, 1995), p. 89.

6. Ibid.

7. Carol F. Karlsen, *The Devil in the Shape of a Woman* (New York: Norton, 1987), pp. 12–13.

8. Hill, p. 166.

9. Ibid., p. 100.

10. Starkey, p. 160.

11. Hill, p. 167.

12. Ibid.

13. Anne Llewellyn Barstow, *Witchcraze* (New York: HarperCollins, 1994), p. 78.

Chapter 2. A Religious Colony

1. John Winthrop, "A Model of Christian Charity," *Winthrop Papers* (Boston: The Massachusetts Historical Society, 1931), vol. II, p. 295.

2. Peter Charles Hoffer, *The Devil's Disciples* (Baltimore: Johns Hopkins University Press, 1996), p. 40.

3. Paul Boyer and Stephen Nissenbaum, *Salem Possessed* (Cambridge, Mass.: Harvard University Press, 1974), p. 40.

4. Ibid., p. 80.

5. Kai T. Erikson, *Wayward Puritans* (New York: John Wiley and Sons, 1966), p. 135.

6. George Francis Dow, *Everyday Life in the Massachusetts Bay Colony* (New York: Dover, 1988), p. 201.

7. Frances Hill, *A Delusion of Satan* (New York: Doubleday, 1995), p. 10.

8. Anne Llewellyn Barstow, *Witchcraze* (New York: HarperCollins, 1994), p. 39.

9. Boyer and Nissenbaum, pp. 192–193.

10. James Heath, *Torture and English Law* (Westport, Conn.: Greenwood, 1982), pp. 169–170.

11. Hill, p. 11.

12. J. G. Bellamy, *Criminal Law and Society in Late Medieval and Tudor England* (New York: St. Martin's Press, 1984), p. 143.

13. Elaine G. Breslaw, *Tituba, Reluctant Witch of Salem* (New York: New York University Press, 1996), p. 108.

14. Hill, p. 162.

15. Richard Weisman, *Witchcraft, Magic, and Religion in 17th Century Massachusetts* (Amherst, Mass.: University of Massachusetts Press, 1984), p. 13.

16. Carol F. Karlsen, *The Devil in the Shape of a Woman* (New York: Norton, 1987), p. 21.

17. Ibid.

18. John Putnam Demos, *Entertaining Satan* (London: Oxford University Press, 1982), p. 93.

19. Barstow, p. 127.

20. Hill, p. 16.

21. Ibid.

22. Breslaw, p. 115.

23. Karlsen, p. 34.

Chapter 3. The Trouble Begins

1. Richard Godbeer, *The Devil's Dominion* (Cambridge: Cambridge University Press, 1992), p. 5.

2. Paul Boyer and Stephen Nissenbaum, *Salem Possessed* (Cambridge, Mass.: Harvard University Press, 1974), pp. 45–56.

3. Peter Charles Hoffer, *The Devil's Disciples* (Baltimore: Johns Hopkins University Press, 1996), p. 59.

4. Boyer and Nissenbaum, p. 1.

5. Ibid.

6. Ibid.

7. Ibid., p. 2.

8. Frances Hill, *A Delusion of Satan* (New York: Doubleday, 1995), p. 23.

9. Boyer and Nissenbaum, p. 2.

10. Hill, p. 27.

11. Ibid., p. 24.

12. Boyer and Nissenbaum, pp. 4–5.

13. Ibid.

14. Hill, p. 47.

15. Ibid., p. 48.

16. Ibid.

17. Elaine G. Breslaw, *Tituba, Reluctant Witch of Salem* (New York: New York University Press, 1996), p. 122.

18. Hill, p. 50.

19. Ibid., p. 51.

20. Ibid., p. 77.

21. Ibid.

22. Ibid., p. 161.

23. Hill, p. 93.

24. Marian L. Starkey, *The Devil in Massachusetts* (New York: Doubleday, 1949), p. 93.

25. Hoffer, p. 123.

26. Starkey, p. 82.

27. Ibid., p. 83.

28. Ibid.

29. Ibid., p. 84.

30. Enders A. Robinson, *The Devil Discovered* (New York: Hippocrene, 1991), p. 1.

31. Starkey, p. 157.

Chapter 4. The Accusers

1. Frances Hill, *A Delusion of Satan* (New York: Doubleday, 1995), p. 154.

2. Enders Robinson, *The Devil Discovered* (New York: Hippocrene, 1991), p. 127.

3. John Putnam Demos, *Entertaining Satan* (London: Oxford University Press, 1982), p. 173.

4. Carol F. Karlsen, *The Devil in the Shape of a Woman* (New York: Norton, 1987), p. 171.

5. Anne Llewellyn Barstow, *Witchcraze* (New York: HarperCollins, 1994), p. 62.

6. Hill, pp. 20–22.

7. Ibid., p. 92.

8. Lori Lee Wilson, *The Salem Witch Trials* (Minneapolis: Lerner, 1997), p. 58.

9. Ibid., p. 57.

10. Richard B. Trask, *"The Devil Hath Been Raised"* (West Kennebunk, Maine: Phoenix Publishing 1992), p. 118.

11. Ibid.

12. Ibid.

13. Ibid.

14. Hill, p. 151.

15. Paul Boyer and Stephen Nissenbaum, *Salem Possessed* (Cambridge, Mass.: Harvard University Press, 1974), p. 104.

16. Ibid., p. 189.

17. Ibid.

18. Ibid., p. 90.

19. Ibid., p. 102.

20. Ibid.

21. Ibid., p. 186.

22. Robinson, p. 40.

23. Ibid., pp. 37–38.

24. Hill, p. 39.

25. Elaine G. Breslaw, *Tituba, Reluctant Witch of Salem* (New York: New York University Press, 1996), p. 72.

26. Hill, p. 40.

Chapter 5. The Accused

1. Richard B. Trask, *"The Devil Hath Been Raised"* (West Kennebunk, Maine: Phoenix Publishing 1992), p. 110.

2. Carol F. Karlsen, *The Devil in the Shape of a Woman* (New York: W. W. Norton, 1987), p. 47.

3. Ibid., p. 48.

4. Ibid., pp. 64–65.

5. Ibid., p. 75.

6. Ibid., p. 104.

7. John Putnam Demos, *Entertaining Satan* (London: Oxford University Press, 1982), p. 93.

8. Karlsen, p. 156.

9. Laurel Thatcher Ulrich, *Good Wives* (New York: Knopf, 1982), p. 6.

10. Paul Boyer and Stephen Nissenbaum, *Salem Possessed* (Cambridge, Mass.: Harvard University Press, 1974), p. 26.

11. Ibid.

12. Ibid., p. 208.

13. Frances Hill, *A Delusion of Satan* (New York: Doubleday, 1995), p. 67.

14. Marion L. Starkey, *The Devil in Massachusetts* (New York: Doubleday, 1949), p. 141.

15. Ibid.

16. Boyer and Nissenbaum, p. 9.
17. Ibid., pp. 7–8.
18. Lori Lee Wilson, *The Salem Witch Trials* (Minneapolis: Lerner, 1997), p. 31.
19. Trask, p. 107.
20. Ibid.
21. The Bible, King James Version, John 6:70.
22. Trask, p. 110.
23. Hill, p. 179.
24. Boyer and Nissenbaum, p. 12.
25. Hill, p. 179.
26. Ibid., p. 183.
27. Trask, p. 11.
28. Hill, p. 138.
29. Chadwick Hansen, *Witchcraft at Salem* (New York: George Braziller, 1969), p. 111.
30. Enders A. Robinson, *The Devil Discovered* (New York: Hippocrene, 1991), p. 238.
31. Hill, p. 148.
32. Richard Weisman, *Witchcraft, Magic, and Religion in 17th Century Massachusetts* (Amherst, Mass.: University of Massachusetts Press, 1984), p. 157.
33. Hill, p. 137.
34. Boyer and Nissenbaum, p. 210.
35. Robinson, p. 7.

Chapter 6. The Verdict

1. Kai T. Erikson, *Wayward Puritans* (New York: John Wiley and Sons, 1966), p. 158.
2. Marion L. Starkey, *The Devil in Massachusetts* (New York: Doubleday, 1949), p. 161.
3. Frances Hill, *A Delusion of Satan* (New York: Doubleday, 1995), p. 185.
4. Starkey, p. 75.
5. Peter Charles Hoffer, *The Devil's Disciples* (Baltimore: Johns Hopkins University Press, 1996), p. xi.

6. Ibid.

7. Hill, p. 132.

8. Ibid., p. 111.

9. Starkey, p. 249.

10. Ibid., p. 220.

11. Chadwick Hansen, *Witchcraft at Salem* (New York: George Braziller, 1969), p. 104.

12. Paul Boyer and Stephen Nissenbaum, *Salem Possessed* (Cambridge, Mass.: Harvard University Press, 1974), p. 10.

13. Starkey, p. 220.

14. Hill, p. 215.

15. Elaine G. Breslaw, *Tituba, Reluctant Witch of Salem* (New York: New York University Press, 1996), p. 175.

16. Richard Weisman, *Witchcraft, Magic, and Religion in 17th Century Massachusetts* (Amherst, Mass.: University of Massachusetts Press, 1984), p. 209.

17. Starkey, p. 267.

18. Ibid.

19. Lori Lee Wilson, *The Salem Witch Trials* (Minneapolis: Lerner, 1997), p. 55.

20. Ibid., p. 51.

21. Richard Godbeer, *The Devil's Dominion, Magic and Religion in Early New England* (Cambridge: Cambridge University Press, 1992), p. 223.

22. Hill, p. 215.

23. Ibid., p. 207.

24. Ibid.

25. Starkey, p. 268.

Chapter 7. The Aftermath

1. Richard Godbeer, *The Devil's Dominion, Magic and Religion in Early New England* (Cambridge: Cambridge University Press, 1992), p. 224.

2. John Putnam Demos, *Entertaining Satan* (London: Oxford University Press, 1982), p. 392.

3. Ibid.

4. Frances Hill, *A Delusion of Satan* (New York: Doubleday, 1995), p. 205.

5. United States Constitution, First Amendment.

6. *Everson* v. *Board of Education*, 330 U.S. 1 (1947).

7. Ibid.

8. Ibid.

9. James L. Hutson, *Religion and the Founding of the American Republic* (Washington, D.C.: Library of Congress, 1998), p. 85.

10. Joseph McCarthy, "The Internal Communist Menace," *A History of Our Time* (New York: Oxford University Press, 1995), pp. 63–64.

11. Ibid.

12. Ethan Bronner, "Witching Hour," *The New York Times*, October 18, 1998, section 4, p. 1.

Glossary

afflicted girls—Term used by the residents of Salem during the witch trials to refer to the supposed victims of witchcraft. The term was used even though many of the alleged victims were adults.

charter—The legal document in which the British king or queen granted an American colony the right to exist. The charter explained the conditions under which the colony was to be governed.

Court of Oyer and Terminer—The court of "hearing and deciding" that tried the witchcraft cases in Salem.

General Court—The highest authority in Massachusetts, combining some of the functions of today's United States Supreme Court and Congress. The General Court passed laws and decided points of law.

goodwife—The title of some respect given to an ordinary married woman in Puritan society. Abbreviated as "goody."

hysteria—A psychological state in which the behavior and emotions of a person are out of control. The person knows what he or she is doing but is unable to control the actions.

McCarthyism—A term describing the behavior of Senator Joseph McCarthy, whose anti-Communist crusade of the 1950s has been compared to the Salem witch trials.

meeting—The Puritan religious service.

Puritans—A popular name for members of the Congregationalist Church, given because the Puritans wanted to "purify" the Church of England.

specter—A spirit or ghost of a living person, sent out of the body to another place.

spectral evidence—Descriptions of the activities of a specter, visible only to the victim of the specter's actions.

stocks—A wooden frame that was used for locking the body of a criminal into one position. The stocks were used as punishment in colonial Salem.

theocracy—A government in which one religion is recognized as official. The government and religion are intertwined and share power.

touch test—A test to discover witchcraft. If a victim touches a witch, the spell is supposed to flow back into the witch, whereupon the victim is cured.

visible saints—Puritans admitted to full membership in their church. They were called visible saints because their behavior was said to show that they were destined for heaven.

water test—A test to discover a witch. Since it was believed that a witch would float, a person who sank when tossed in the water was believed to be innocent.

witchcraze—Term used by some historians to describe a time in which many witchcraft trials were held.

witch's teat—A mark on a witch's body, believed to be a sign of the devil.

Further Reading

Fremon, David K. *The Salem Witchcraft Trials in American History*. Springfield, N.J.: Enslow Publishers, Inc., 1999.

Hill, Frances. *A Delusion of Satan*. New York: Doubleday, 1995.

Kent, Deborah. *Salem, Massachusetts*. Parsippany, N.J.: Silver Burdett Press, 1995.

Roach, Marilynne K. *In the Days of the Salem Witchcraft Trials*. New York: Ticknor & Fields, 1996.

Stein, Wendy. *Witches*. San Diego, Calif.: Greenhaven, 1995.

Trask, Richard B. *"The Devil Hath Been Raised": A Documentary History of the Salem Witchcraft Outbreak of March 1692*. West Kennebunk, Maine: Phoenix Publishing, 1992.

Van der Linde, Laurel. *The Devil in Salem Village: The Story of the Salem Witchcraft Trials*. Brookfield, Conn: Millbrook Press, Inc. 1992.

Internet Addresses

National Geographic's Salem Information
<http://www.nationalgeographic.com/features/97/salem/
index.html>

**Famous American Trials: Salem Witchcraft Trials,
1962**
<http://www.law.umkc.edu/faculty/projects/ftrials/salem/
salem.htm>

**The Colonial Gazette: MayFlower, Massachusetts
and New England Events**
<http://www.mayflowerfamilies.com/enquirer>

Index